MAKING
CHRISTIAN
SENSE

SPIRITUALITY AND THE CHRISTIAN LIFE
Richard H. Bell, *Editor*

MAKING CHRISTIAN SENSE

PAUL L. HOLMER

THE WESTMINSTER PRESS
Philadelphia

BOOK DESIGN BY ALICE DERR

First edition

Published by The Westminster Press®
Philadelphia, Pennsylvania

PRINTED IN THE UNITED STATES OF AMERICA
2   4   6   8   9   7   5   3   1

Library of Congress Cataloging in Publication Data

Holmer, Paul L.
  Making Christian sense.

  (Spirituality and the Christian life series)
  1. Christian life—1960–   . I. Title. II. Series.
BV4501.2.H567 1984   248.4   83-27373
ISBN 0-664-24614-1 (pbk.)

TO RANDALL

CONTENTS

ACKNOWLEDGMENTS

These pages were written to show that the Christian teachings, though they are indeed objective and are found in theologies, liturgies, the Bible, and sermons, yet are also adverbial. That is, they are only appreciated and understood when they begin to modify all of us, and in deep ways. So we can be changed and even converted—emotionally, morally, and in will and thought. This makes for the chief theme of this book.

But I owe much more than I can ever be owed for whatever graces these pages. Kierkegaard, Wittgenstein, David Swenson, and Herbert Feigl have been spies in the service of ideas and have forced me to cope in unexpected ways. Beyond that I owe my sister, Joyce Gustafson, a great deal. She not only typed these pages but she made me re-say and re-think all kinds of lines and paragraphs. So I thank her, too, for friendly helps.

The dedication of these pages is to my brother, who, amid lifelong hurts and distress, has forced me to a first-hand awareness that through all things we still can be conquerors through Jesus Christ, who loves us all.

P.L.H.

EDITOR'S INTRODUCTION

In 1609 Francis de Sales published a helpful book designed "to instruct those who live in town, within families, or at court, and by their state of life are obliged to live an ordinary life." It was, as he said, "a collection of bits of good advice stated in plain, intelligible words." The book, *Introduction to the Devout Life*, became a "spiritual classic." Although we will not claim that the books in this series will become spiritual classics, they are intended for a similar reader—one "obliged to live an ordinary life"—and they are written in "plain, intelligible words."

In terms of their subject matter, they share another point with Francis de Sales's book. He said about the Christian life that "a strong, resolute soul can live in the world without being infected by any of its moods." This was not an easy task then, nor is it now. But one of the goals of the Christian life is to free ourselves from circumstances that hinder love and service to God. When the apostle Paul spoke of having the "mind of Christ," he was asking that we not yield to the accidental features of this world; that we strive to free ourselves from being defined by the social, political, and economic contingencies of this world. A great effort of the spirit is needed to do this.

This series is intended to help its readers in this effort of the spirit. We call these books spiritual because they deal with how God's Spirit intersects with the human spirit. They focus attention on the *Bible* as the principal source for hearing and understanding God's Spirit, and on the *self* as the agent for living in the spirit.

Again, Francis de Sales suggests a strategy that augurs well for the volumes in this series. He asks: "How can we fight against [our imperfections] unless we see them, or overcome them unless we face them?" And he answers: "Our victory does not consist in being unconscious of them but in not consenting to them, and not to consent to them is to be displeased with them." Growth in the spirit involves seeing and facing our imperfections, not consenting to them; it involves being displeased with them and having courage to suffer the wounds meted out by our world. Such growth is given its Christian shape by our memories and stories, by our inner life in its emptiness and fullness, its weakness and strength, as we relate to God as Emmanuel—"God with us." In this concept of *God with us* the series finds its foundation in what is traditionally called *spirituality*.

But more important in this series is how we come to discern God with us and activate our will to make sense of our lives. Thus a second focus is that of building character and its natural outflow in the life of a Christian. The Christian life comes down to how each person faithfully lives in the human community and makes that great effort of spirit in devotion to God and in daily moral and political service.

If no other books you have read lately have encouraged you to take hold of your self and your Christian life with courage and firmness, these books will. They will take you patiently through many identifiable thickets of human life and ask you when it was that you allowed God to speak to you, embrace you, and lead you. These books are intended to be traveling companions, guides to take you closer to the center of the Christian life, closer to the Bible, closer to yourself, and thus, it is hoped, closer to God.

In this book, MAKING CHRISTIAN SENSE, Paul L. Holmer starts by asking how we can make sense of our lives. This, he says, is a task for which we seem "woefully un-prepared." While we are surrounded on the one hand by relative peace and plenty, and on the other by poverty and violence, the striking thing about our life as human beings is that we seem no closer to happiness and no more threat-ened by social problems than others were in other ages. But in our time, unlike some other times, we do lack some es-sentials for our life. We lack a certain rest for our souls and seem far from understanding what it means to be a person nurtured by the Christian faith. To address these difficulties, Holmer proposes that making sense in a Christian way "can be done by fashioning distinctive Christian emotions, by considering new virtues, by finding a new power and shape for the will, and also by making a kind of sense in thought and belief with the new mind available to us in Christ Je-sus."

On the surface, this volume, when compared with others in the series, may appear to be the most remote from tradi-tional "spirituality," but the truth is that Holmer pays very close attention to our "lack of spiritual health" (our "being lost") and to our deep need for cure. What surfaces in his pages, time and again, is the notion that the Christian faith can provide the cure and can help us to make sense of our lives. It can provide us with some wants that we won't out-live or outspend, and with some hopes that will tie things together and not "wither away under the stress of daily life." "Most of us," says Holmer, "have hardly any concept of God at all, barely even an image or a vague intimation. But the exercise of hope in one's life, letting deep feelings grow as one centers down into steadfastness and patience, will cause the very idea of God to take root." Also to nurture our emo-tions, our virtues, our will, and our thought in Christian ways is to form our lives as faithful servants of our Lord.

Finally, Holmer says that, en route to understanding the

Christian story, "we must also live in the grace and the new motives that the story promises." And it is this "living in"— the *how* of our being Christians—and the nurturing of the "new motives," which are found in our emotions, our virtue, our will, and our thoughts, that are so carefully detailed in this book. If, in fact, we fail to discover these new motives in our sojourn with Christianity, then "it must be that we have not understood the story."

RICHARD H. BELL

CHAPTER ONE

MAKING SENSE
OF OUR LIVES

I

These pages are penned with the thought that our lives must make a certain kind of sense. But making sense with one's life is not nearly as easy as making sense of one's speech. We are all used to the thought that if we babble on, and if what we say is only a jumble of noise, then something is seriously wrong. We agree that we ought to talk sense. A string of words, merely spelled correctly but fitting no aim or purpose does not make for sense either. Again, we all know that a little grammar, some knowledge of what we are speaking or writing about, and certainly a feel for the fittingness of our remarks, will help us avoid nonsense and keep our words from being foolish and pointless.

Most of us who have thought about this at all are aware of rules, techniques, teachers, and a variety of other available helps. We use examples, traditions, disciplines, and various kinds of training to aid us. None of us has to experiment and do all this for the first time. Instead, a kind of confidence grows with the precedents so that we mostly need to submit ourselves to what has gone on before and is going on now around us in order to learn what is necessary.

With our lives, everything seems to be different. With all

our energies, activities, and potentialities, we are far less sure of ourselves. Most of us fit easily with the popular thought that our lives ought to be vivid and bright, zestful and full of spirit. Perhaps we would like to be carefree, exuberant, and even extravagant in manner. However, we soon learn, often to our dismay, that living a human life like that is almost impossible; that daily life is very exacting, often plainly tiring; and that our lives are dull, too short, and certainly never easy.

More than this, we soon begin to judge our lives as a whole. We often do not like what we have made of ourselves. This peculiar sense that we develop of ourselves is not just a record of the incidents through which we have lived or of the situations we have either liked or merely endured. Rather it is a kind of awareness that all those days, events, deeds through which we have lived ought to hang together, and that being alive as a person is to put them all together in some kind of fashion. It is almost as if we are not just breathing and existing but are also making ourselves as we go. So the stakes get rather high. Furthermore, because we live only once, we do not have the chance to practice the story for ourselves.

Sometimes we get a dramatic sense of the self that has been made by all this. It looks, occasionally, as if things are adding up and that there is a person there, after all, of whom we can be moderately proud. But at other times we succumb to an anxious feeling that there is nothing to show for all the effort and turmoil. We do feel then that we are wasting effort and time, that nothing is being accomplished of a fundamental sort. Then it is as if life itself is pointless, as if there is nothing to show for the strain and stress. The way the happenings—maybe our marriage, our job, our way of getting along—have gone together has left us empty and with the dismal thought that we are not any better as a person than we were years before. This is what is meant by saying that we begin to think about our lives as a whole, as a self.

How helpless we sometimes feel here! On this very important matter of how to live, rather than how to speak or write, we all tend to flounder. Furthermore, popular opinion of the day will have it that each must do it alone. So there is a skepticism in literature and smart magazine talk to the effect that our age is so different from earlier times that the wisdom of the past is also dated. Even if we read early literature, the apostles or the Greeks, Shakespeare or Jesus' words, we seem always to be lost in interpretations, and never is there much that is clear and unambiguous. The result is that we become cynical about advice, contemptuous of examples, and sneering toward any teacher who proposes to teach a way of life. We live as if being modern has doomed us all to a kind of blind experimentation.

Making sense of our lives, then, is quite different from making sense in a conversation or being reasonable in an argument. But it is not so desperate a difference as is often asserted. We do not have to experiment endlessly, nor do we have to leave everything to chance. Altogether too many people settle only for making money or for being acceptable to other people. Developing a kind of marketing orientation for oneself, whereby one makes oneself desirable, beautiful, or salable, is a kind of proneness that any of us can exploit; but it is usually short-lived and breeds an even deeper cynicism. For the market keeps changing too. What worked at the age of twenty does not matter at the age of forty. Yet a lot of what we learn about living is like that. Sometimes we need money and lots of it, or youthfulness that is never-ending, or an endless array of things and baubles to keep ourselves pertinent and abreast. All this is part of the disease called worldliness; it is not the cure. No wonder, then, that the sorrows of life begin to mount up, sometimes even through a lifetime.

Making sense of a life admittedly cannot be done from the

outside. So no one can provide you with all the conditions. Here we have to remember an analogy with ordinary talking. We always have to ask, of even the most clear and cogent set of remarks, at least one question, namely, "Who said that?", for words need a speaker. It is always a speaker who makes sense with the words. As we have noted already, there are rules and teachers here. Furthermore it is not correct to say, on the more momentous issues of how to live, that there is no teaching or that there are no teachers. The person who helps you make sense in talking does so by drawing on the many-sided and very informal grammar of our language and the equally complex and equally informal logic of our daily thought. These are embedded in human practices, in literature and ways of speaking; and they are not arbitrary, nor are they invented by the teacher.

Something like this obtains also in the other domain to which we have been referring. There is a kind of logic, and perhaps we can also call it a grammar of living, too. It is not the same in every respect as the easier grammar of language, but the important fact to note here is that the teachers of wisdom have usually not been inventors of the grammar of life as much as they have been commentators upon it. The point is that it is there and can be drawn upon. We are not quite as hopeless and bereft as popular culture makes us appear. Nor is that wisdom of the past only an echo of another culture; nor is it the vehicle for dogmatic authoritarians trying to thwart the moderns. On the contrary, just as knowing the rules of language enables one to use it well, so knowing the wisdom of life enables one to live adventurously and even well.

But there will be more of this in later pages. We began by saying that making sense of one's life is an awesome task, one for which most of us seem woefully unprepared. Sometimes even the Christian churches and the priests and ministers seem unable to address these issues, except by conforming to the main themes in contemporary social life. Part of the difficulty does seem to lie in hasty and shallow diagnoses of the difficulties. So in this chapter I propose to sketch those conditions which make us painfully aware of the senselessness and meaninglessness of our lives. They are several in kind. In what is said, I am being bold in thinking that the social conditions to which we so often are urged to pay attention, namely, poverty, war, inequities of several kinds, and so forth, are not as decisive in creating a meaningless life as other conditions to which I will allude. We have said that much contemporary religion and morality is superficially conceived and discussed. Part of what was meant is that the social conditions are obvious and simply loom up before us, demand attention, and, subsequently, receive inflated importance on this issue of the quality of our lives just because they are there and are so plain.

We do have to remember that social conditions affect and hurt us in a variety of ways. But there are other conditions that are often more subtle and devastating. Also, they are more difficult and painful to think about. For whether we live in poverty or plenty, we are still subject to anxiety; whether we live in slavery or freedom, we are still prone to guilt; in either war or peace we still suffer from weakness and indecisiveness. Somehow the proximity and plainness of the advantages of prosperity, of peace, and of freedom make us want to exaggerate their advantages and attribute to them a healing of the spirit that they can never bring. For amid all the advantages of contemporary life, where fewer people suffer disease, hunger, or lack of opportunities than in years past, there still is probably no increase in the sum total of human happiness and very slight advantage, if any, in the main business of making sense of one's life.

Because all of us can do something about social conditions, namely, talk about them, design policies, or organize causes around them, we also are prone to think that therein are the necessary conditions for the good life and even the Christian life. But this produces new delusions, a deeply mistaken notion of what a human life is and needs, and also a mistaken set of conceptions about the moral life and what Christianity is. This is not to deny the attractiveness of social goals, for we owe a great deal to the enlightened interests of those who have made contemporary living healthier, easier, more prosperous, and conducive to a variety of freedoms. But these too are obvious and need very slight defense.

What is not so plain is just how we establish ourselves as persons. How do we get a peace that passes all understanding? How do we get rest for our souls? In living our lives, we have a right still to the task of achieving a profound and responsible happiness. The kind of questing that goes on in all persons for a kind of certainty about oneself, a sense of satisfaction that all is well, is not met by any one set of social or economic conditions. Furthermore, it cannot be met by general policies, nor can it be done to you by a benevolent government or an up-to-date religious institution. The vicissitudes of being a person are still with us. On the other side we have the claims of religious and moral teachings. They seem to be addressed to human conditions that stay somewhat the same, despite the transitions to industrialism, to the age of science, to wider worlds and never-ending novelties. Clearly, Christian teachings propose an eternal and abiding significance. Mediating between restless and changing humankind and eternal verities is the task of every preacher and every religious teacher.

Briefly, then, we are here turning to the human condition and looking at those features of it which warrant our judgment that our lives are not making sense. By seeing these we hope to find also the junctures, the points of correspondence, between ourselves and the teachings of the Christian faith and of the Bible. In subsequent chapters we shall propose that making sense in a Christian way can be done by fashioning distinctive Christian emotions, by considering new virtues, by finding a new power and shape for the will, and also by making a kind of sense in thought and belief with the new mind available to us in Christ Jesus.

In another respect, these remarks have to do with the pragmatics, the common ways in which all of us have to make use of Christian teachings. For in the past century or two, Christian literature and practices have been studied with all the best tools of learning and by literally battalions of scholars and students. The result is a vast and unwieldy technical literature, easily available to anyone who wants to consult it. But all this has multiplied the detail of the "what," the subject matter of the Christian and Jewish religions. As for the "how" of its use and assimilation to the task of building up a distinctive Christian mind; a tough and resilient moral passion to cope Christianly with the world; a depiction of the suppleness and deftness of the human spirit— these and more have not improved in the least, despite the talk about psychology, counseling, and being people-oriented. Most of us fail as persons and make disasters of our lives because of defects of will, the poverty and shallowness of our emotions, a lack of practical wisdom, or even because we do not like or take pleasure in what we ought.

So these pages draw our attention both to the broken and contrite heart, on the one side, and to the new heart and mind that results from Christian nurture, on the other.

II

We are sketching here only a few of the conditions that make our living seem senseless and almost without point. First, and typical, I believe, is the condition of a person who cannot get out of the persistent affective complexes that we call moods. (Later we will have occasion to distinguish more sharply among moods, passions, attitudes, feelings, sentiments, and emotions, but here we will speak more generally about these affective states under the label "emotions.") If you are always in a state of wrath, so that anger is constant no matter what happens, then the world around you takes on a single coloration. Everything makes you mad; everything is in a single lump. Soon there are no highs and no lows, and there is no respite in how things turn out. Nothing much matters then; because everything looks about the same, your attempts at making a go of things look like vanity.

This is the way it is, too, with a vengeful attitude. If we have so judged ourselves and others that we always have to get even, then this vengefulness destroys all equanimity and peace of mind. We begin to look at the world more harshly, and nothing is right until this overriding need for getting even is met. Usually it never is, so we are left with a skewed and harsh world, alien to the way things really are. Once more, we ourselves and the world around us are a poor fit. It is all very well to try to remake the world to fit oneself, but anger and vengefulness are not usually very good clues as to where to begin. In the cases above, anger and vengefulness, like general anxiety and sadness, are not simple responses to the way the world or events are. Instead, they are clues to the way we are.

Consider anger that is directed toward an object, be it a person or an action. There is a difference—a sharp one—between anger that is deserved and appropriate and anger that is continuous and unabated no matter what transpires. The first anger can even be right, whereas the second loses discrimination and never is quite right. It is the second kind of emotion that can make life meaningless. We slip into those dreadful periods, and we let the ambiguous world and the moral haziness of ourselves and other people keep feeding our unhappy moods. The world around us is often poorly defined, and people are surely halfhearted and often fools. We do not have to look far or hard to see that colleagues, husbands, wives, bosses, or our children have their foibles and, besides, even seem to like their foolishness. It is not hard to keep anger going in such a world. But think of the price you pay for keeping it going. This proneness to be mad about something is like tinder that bursts into flame altogether too easily.

When we allow ourselves to be like that, we are clear illustrations of what New Testament authors mean about being sinners. For sin is also the name for that "tinder," that inclination we all harbor for wrath. Not only are we likely to flare up and strike out at others, but living our lives then becomes a terrible burden. If anything makes a life seem empty and vain, it is that awful feeling that we cannot cope with the business of living. For to do it so badly that we are always in turmoil is to make it almost intolerable.

Sadness can do this for us too. When everything looks like a tragedy, even before we try it, we can be sure that a kind of melancholic sadness has been there first. There are legitimate reasons for sadness. Certainly, sensitive people grieve long and do not forget quickly. We even have good cause to praise those who have loved so deeply and so well that they do not love quickly again; instead, their memory of one who is lost stays with them, and they take solace mostly in the memory. There are surely a variety of cases here. But sadness that goes on becomes after a while another way to blur the world and one's own deeds. If you always have tears in your eyes, you cannot see much of anything clearly.

The point here, however, is to pay attention to our lack of spiritual health. Sometimes our emotions are the chief symptoms. If we are always fearful, then it is as if every moment of life puts us in jeopardy. This is what happens to us when anxiety floats from one issue to another, and again we get no rest anywhere. What might have started out as a genuine fear of this or that can be fed, almost from within, so that an anxiety about everything can ensue. Then nothing much makes sense for us, for no matter where we turn, desperation and wretchedness seem exactly right.

The popular talk of our day, even contemporary psychology, will cause us to handle these issues as if the emotions themselves were the sickness. Sometimes psychotherapy and psychoanalysis have looked like new and scientific ways to handle such matters, almost as if reeducating our moral life and our emotions, and becoming converted by Jesus Christ, were old-fashioned and doomed to another age. So we have been told to relive our past, to discover our own drives, to realize our individuality, to free ourselves from conflicts, parents, and social pressures. Indeed, there may be cases in which diagnoses like these are on target, but they must be exceptions and not the rule. For what we can read of the grammar of life tells us also that we must make sense of our life, not just once but from day to day. One way to fail in living is to let moods like anxiety, anger, melancholy, and (surely the worst of all) despair pervade our sensibilities.Then the whole of life gets a very dull cast, and it begins to look as if all effort is pointless.

This is to draw our attention, then, to a fact about moral and Christian cultivation: chiefly, that it is not a bit of woolgathering and a matter of optional pleasantries. Despite big differences between morality and Christianity, the fact is that both are also disciplines that aim at providing a cure for the lack of emotions as well as a pattern for new emotions. Part of the sense-making that Christianity provides is a whole panoply of new emotions. Hope, fear of the Lord, contrition about oneself, love—these and more are not just variations of the familiar or permutations on something we already have, they are new affects, new forms of pathos.

III

What we have said about the emotions can be paralleled by remarks about some other forms of character that we call virtues. This is a second area in which we often fail to make sense. We will note here again some typical ways of living that make lives meaningless.

Previously we said that anger can start as an emotion

about this or that, often deserved, and yet end up as a smoldering kind of wrath about almost everything. Indignation can become a habit and tell us after a while more about the person than about the things he or she is indignant over. For this very reason, morality long since took notice and began to call this kind of anger a vice, and the name "wrath" was reserved for this habitual mode of responding. Few people who suffer wrath really enjoy it, so it is not long before a conscience on this matter begins to develop.

Two ways loom up once one tries to gather one's thoughts about what is necessary for a truly human mode of living. For one thing, we all need some well-established dispositions, some tested proclivities, to carry us through. Wrath is not one of them. Neither can we improvise every minute. We need preparation and discipline just to get on with meeting the countless circumstances that come our way. We already have some patterned ways of coping with many superficial needs. We are prepared in a habitual way to say "Good morning," to be polite, to take care of a host of physical needs; and most of these neither need nor have any elaborate justification. But virtues are names for these long-standing and powerful dispositions, these tendencies to act in certain ways, that affect large areas of our behavior. If we do not have them, we usually cannot manage our lives very well. So the first need is clearly for habitual character traits. As the early Greek philosophers noted, and as others have seen since, we need courage habitually, not just once, to cope with the happenings of the world; a sense of justice, not just now and then but always, to be able to treat others fairly; temperance, to avoid the catastrophes that usually adhere to doing things in extreme; and a kind of prudential and trained mind that will promise wisdom rather than folly.

But the absence of sense-making is seen right here, for if we have no trained responses at all, we become the victims of circumstances, never the masters. If one has few or no acquired dispositions, then one is without any inhibitions, which means one has no character. Worse than that, to be without character is like being without form, without obligation, and surely also without a true self. One has little to give oneself identity, nothing by which to make sense, nothing to know or to cherish. However, this kind of meaninglessness is matched by another and related way of describing persons, especially when a life is dominated by a vice like wrath, or lust, or covetousness. This is the second way of thinking about ourselves. All of us must avoid habits and dispositions that make us wretched. Vices are, indeed, habits, but their effect is baleful, seldom helpful. What we noted earlier about wrath can now be entertained again. Wrath, if it is habitual, after a bit makes nonsensical the person who exercises it. All the nuances of daily life get lost when you are continually angry, and all the personal capacities that are delicate and careful get swallowed up. So it is, too, with most vices. They smudge the person and deface the actual world.

If one thinks about making sense with one's person, then the very quality of one's life is what matters. One is asking that one's life be justified, that it make sense, that people, not sentences, be vindicated. To fail at that is to fail at no single thing; likewise, to succeed at it is not to make sense of one's life in and by itself. For this is not a single arena, the sense-making arena. Instead, we make sense emotionally, morally, volitionally, and intellectually. Also, we do not just fail in general. If we did, there would not be much possibility of redemption. For just as we fail to make sense by having no emotions or by having unwarranted ones, so we fail to make sense of ourselves by having no habits or by having vices rather than virtues dominate us. But the cure is also often piecemeal and hence possible.

As we have already noted, recent diagnoses of the moral failures of humankind are usually couched in large policy terms. It is as if we see the large-scale policies to be either wrong or nonexistent. So Christians, too, seem to think that with the right general policy (the right politics), everything will fall into place for each person. We ask for integration of people, for equal opportunities, for rights for everyone, for peace, not war—apparently assuming that the advantage for all will spell sense for each. But persons do not fit that scheme. Neither does personal morality, and neither, for that matter, does Christian teaching. A life is soon misspent and self-defeating when vices dominate. And it does not matter very much whether one is poor or rich, talented or plain, educated or uneducated. After a while, the person who is intemperate loses all character and all confidence. One becomes a kind of spiritual waif, driven by one's own desires. Anxieties multiply, and one begins to feel that living gets one nowhere. Furthermore, no one has to read a vast literature in order to know that ravages of conscience can then set in. Any one of us can bear witness to a very tender capacity, that of being our own censor and judge. Early in our life it begins to show itself. To live satisfactorily, we also need our own self-approval. When self-condemnation grows, an anguish sets in too. The worse condemnation becomes, the more wretched we find ourselves. As the New Testament tells us, laws, ideals, hopes, the very will of God, plus vices and failures, will make our judgments of ourselves very painful.

Undoubtedly there are persons who suffer a stricken conscience for causes that are not justified. But such cases must be fairly rare. Most of us deserve our own rebukes. The question soon becomes whether or not we can bear up for very long. Because it is so painful, we all develop dodges to protect ourselves. We tell ourselves that we are no worse than others, that we just have a tender conscience, that we are too preoccupied with ourselves, and so on. But we are ill advised to take such notions with seriousness. Except for highly dramatic cases, where the conscience has been malformed by very odd circumstances, one's conscience is a veritable link with a deep and significant life. It is not for naught that the author of Ecclesiastes says that he has seen the business of humankind and noted that God has planted the eternal in every person's mind (Eccl. 3). The conscience is like that.

Little wonder, then, that life becomes unbearable when conscience is always thwarted. Even the most secular of moralists in times past knew that only a moral reform could keep a life going. Christians have often agreed, but they also added another, somber note about persons needing forgiveness for sin, of which the conscience is often unaware, and a righteousness given by God, for which moral reform is not even adequate. But the diagnoses can be the same. A wounded conscience, always vanquished and never healed, spells a life that is meaningless. Even worse, there is a desolation that we suffer if we try to squelch the voice of conscience altogether or if we do not even dare to care about ourselves any longer. Then we have the makings of despair, in which anguish becomes almost voiceless.

Such matters ought not to be too quickly attributed to heredity, or to the notion that "that's how I am," or to the dreadful thought that "the whole of life is hellish anyway, so what's the difference?" Once more, there is a Christian diagnosis. These terrors of living are the very stuff of both the Old Testament and the New. Somehow modern Christendom has become polite and bourgeois, and social proprieties have become the matrix for the faith of the apostles. The kinds of personality here noted seem now to be immediately resigned to the radically secular kinds of therapy, but another kind of conceptual system of cause and effect, treatment and prognosis, is readily at hand. It is not mine to say that everything new is wrong or that modern learning is always a diversion, but it is an omission among Christian thinkers if the new life in Christ is not also conceived as a new way to make sense, even morally. And what can make sense is not just talk (for here, too, it is altogether too easy to have all these matters only in one's mouth), but also life itself.

Therefore, as we will note in later chapters, part of the Christian teaching is not information and not more talk. Most of it is training and discipline. Certainly we have to avoid the notion that being a Christian is a matter of works, even a matter of doing this or that and making something of oneself. Instead, faith, even belief, comes first, and the works follow. Another way to see this is to mark that faith in God works itself out in our life stream so that a kind of sense and meaning begins to accrue emotionally as well as morally.

IV

A third diagnosis of a life that begins to falter and to become burdensome is made in terms of the will. We do not have to decide all the difficult issues of what the will is and what the freedom or determinism of the will is in order to note some typical difficulties. When I can no longer exercise myself over my future, when I can no longer decide between opposing options, or when I completely lack wants and wishes, then much of daily life loses its challenge, and I begin to think there is little sense left. The philosopher Aristotle noted long ago that many persons suffer from a weakness of the will.

But a tragedy is in the making when a person does not learn what every person finally must learn: that is, some powerful and persistent wants. For unlike the animals whose wants are given with their very birth and nature, persons have to spend time learning what their proper wants are. And if one does not want what is essential and needful—for example, to be morally sound, to be intelligent and informed rather than stupid, or even to be healthy rather than sick—then a good part of being a person is missing.

No one can live very long without wanting. Wants are not hidden somewhere in one's personality, only needing to be brought into the open. We do not have wants until we start wanting. Once more, this is to make our will operative and deliberate. But this happens only when we begin to activate ourselves; we get wants by wanting and a will by willing. By so doing, we get control of ourselves and also begin to fashion ourselves. We cannot long abide even ourselves, let alone others, if we are will-less; we make living intolerable if no wants keep us shaped and fashioned.

Certainly a person is in dire straits if he or she has to say at the age of fifty or sixty, "I have never known what I wanted." For that state, too, describes a life without any gist, without any significance. Not to know what you want is to be bereft of direction. Typically, a person who does not know what he or she wants may want everything—but nothing for very long. Or such a person wants first this and then that. When trying a job or spending time with a new companion, he or she is quickly bored. A want that is at all substantial survives repetition; it tolerates ordinariness and wins over a host of circumstances. If a person wants to be learned, to get an education, then the force of this want will enable him or her to outlast the competition, to endure long discipline, and even to live, maybe for a long while, without immediate rewards. Without such a want one moves restlessly from one area to another; one tries a large variety of things and nothing satisfies.

Contrary to popular lore, which says "keep trying, you'll find something yet," the fact is that in a large number of cases it is not a question of finding the right person, place, or situation. The issue is not just objective, that is, discovering the right circumstance and then being at rest and eventually satisfied. We are not speaking here of anything whimsical or fanciful, arbitrary or highly personalized. Sometimes our difficulties are that we have not learned the wants that belong to the grammar of human life. If someone wants to play chess badly, even to the extent that he plays seemingly only to lose and never to win, we might find such a person bizarre and surely not one we would care to play with more than once. But playing chess is, after all, a relatively minor matter, and it is strange, although not utterly defacing of one's humanity, to play to lose. Wanting to win at chess is important only for the hours or minutes of the game. But if someone decides to be a cheater, only because he or she prefers cheating—plainly just wants it that way—then we do not know what to say or do. The grammar and limits of life are transgressed.

We have to learn the wants that matter. And here is where the drama of our life begins to manifest itself. A life becomes meaningless and even valueless if wants are not clarified and established. Almost as bad is the life with no wants at all. Then there is no continuity; time is only spent, never redeemed.

All of us know drifters, and maybe some of us fight the tendency to go hither and yon without direction or purpose. We like sometimes to be free and to do things at random! But as our diagnosis shows, it is also true that there is a kind of education of the will that is available for all of us. We can learn powerful and livable wants, wishes, and purposes, and we can, accordingly, give status to ourselves by a will that overcomes vacillation, doubt, and paralysis. We can even like to be purposeful. If we do not, then we are doomed to being ineffectual, uncertain, and perhaps driven always by events and circumstances.

Dare we say that Christianity also brings us up against factors that are worthy of the most powerful passion? Indeed, faith itself is something like a passion. When one is gripped by a zeal for God, and also for righteousness and justice, then it is as if the will is also tutored. Soon we are no longer wanting promiscuously, and we are not just willing at random or by chance. However, the tutoring here is bit by bit; in both the moral life and the Christian life (they do overlap) we learn as we go. Our point is that a large part of sensemaking can be done with our very lives. Much of religious teaching becomes a playful abstraction if we do not realize the ways the will is formed and nurtured. We will turn to more positive aspects of this sense-making in Chapter 4.

V

Now we come to the fourth area where sense is sometimes utterly lost and where it is sometimes also gained: that of the mind. But here I wish to propose a distinction so understanding will not be completely baffled. One of the common things said about Christian teachings is that they are paradoxical or even that they are contradictory. Some say that Christianity is absurd and that it cannot be believed in for that very reason. Others, who are very subtle apologists, say that because it is absurd, even by logical standards, it is therefore distinct and worthy of belief. All kinds of issues are raised in discussing whether the teachings, in and by themselves, make any sense. Many serious thinkers—Tertullian, Augustine, Luther, Kierkegaard, and Barth, among others— have remarked on this aspect of the logic of Christian teachings. For our purposes, we are only going to acknowledge this character of Christian teachings and then go on to another, more personal range of concerns where sense-making is available to us all.

All of us, surely, have to make a kind of sense with our capacities to learn, to argue, to discern, to see—yes, even to think. We have to save and use those capacities. We might summarize our needs as the task of making sense by being aware, by being considerate, by knowing what is what, and, sometimes, by learning why things are as they are. We have to know what is real and what is fantasy, what is fact and what is imagined, what is essential and what is accidental, what is true and what is false. All that put together is a way of saying that every person, granted contrasts in ability and interest, is required to live with big differences. We have to know what is possible and what is only a pipe dream; we have to be capable of seeing what is in the world and what is in oneself; we have to know that everything has limits and that nothing lasts forever. Making sense is a long-time preoccupation, and no one of us ever lives long enough to outlive that need.

The tragedy is that here, too, there are all kinds of disasters in the making. For if we never take the trouble to think, we soon lose a fundamental orientation, one that again belongs to the very logic of existence. Think how sad and how empty is the life of someone only caught up with the present. For if you do not bother to think at all, if you are a misologist (someone who hates to think), you can easily fail to plan for your future. For all of us, there is a future that includes old age, or at least aging, and certainly death. But if we fail to entertain these possibilities and never consider ourselves and our future, we will suddenly discover that both age and death come anyway. Then reality administers a shock, and we are radically unprepared. Again, this is to live an almost meaningless life, one that is harassed by the way things are. Instead of complaining about the realities, we would all be well advised to take them into consideration and live accordingly, marking the difference by a change in awareness of ourselves.

So, too, with the past. We do not have any effective past or future unless we take thought about both. In one sense, of course, we each have a history already, but in another sense we do not have it in any effective and transforming way until we think about it. Once you begin to think about it, a radical reorientation takes place. No longer can you see yourself as self-sufficient. You owe all kinds of things to all kinds of persons. Nothing is quite so much a temptation to lunacy or madness of spirit as the state of being confined to the present moment. We do not even know ourselves if we do not recognize who and what made us. We need desperately an awareness of our transitory and temporary life, so that we measure ourselves in the long sweep of the generations. Then we get a little sanity and a better grip on our daily life.

Another tragedy is in the making when our thought life is only a mad jumble. Here we are not speaking of those who lack formal education or even those who lack the skills of reading and writing. Certainly illiteracy is a serious intellectual flaw, but it is probably not as devastating as we might surmise. Once more, it is fairly easy to teach literacy; both the secularists and the religious are very likely to make grandiose claims about something that most of us can talk about, turn into a cause, and do something about that is definitive and clear. But there is something even more rash and forlorn about the person who can read and write but who has not been the least tempered or assuaged by the skills. Sometimes those very skills multiply the factors one considers and make the jumble pretentious and prideful.

The person who makes sense intellectually has to be disciplined by the world around us. Its prospects, its limits, its potentials, and its powers have to temper our prospects, limits, and powers too. If we do not pay attention to the seasons of our life, we weave a picture for ourselves that will never be realized. If we never pause to know ourselves, we have expectations that are soon fatuous and downright silly. It is not the volume of our knowledge that matters very much, for you can know a great deal about many things and still be an intellectual fool; instead, it is the "how," the way you know, that makes sense of the world and of yourself. That "how" supposes a humility, a sense for the vastness of the unknown, and a clear awareness of how ignorant one is and, more, of how ignorant the whole race is, and how dependent we all are—on forces, on nature, on one another, and ultimately on God Almighty.

The sense that is made for us and with us by our becoming morally serious and becoming a Christian is not something we simply get from books, not even from the Bible. We do not get it in a single lesson. This is a kind of sense that comes when we begin to grasp the rhythm and plan of our own lives and the logic and shape of the world we live in. I am being bold to say that this comes to us piece by piece; but also I insist that it can be learned. We can become adequate to the demands of our existence, though mostly that adequacy is an unmerited, God-given mercy. Still, we begin to surmise this as we believe. We do not get it all at once; we become aware of it as we live according to the teachings of the gospel.

With all these things said, we again venture the more general thought that Christianity is not correctly described unless this breach with practice, both cultural and Christian, is put forward. Christian nurture is not a hobby; it is not designed for the naturally religious; it is not made for those who are making sense already. No, it is for those who have lost their way, for those who are desperate because they cannot put everything together and make their lives truly worthy.

Christian cultivation seeks to give people a new mind that is valiant, brave, and even a little defiant of the flawed creation. It also makes us liable to a purity of heart and a straightening of the will that comes from seeking the one thing needful. It proposes a fear and love of God that will purge us of the vain emotional distresses we usually suffer. Not least, it urges upon us the fruits of the Spirit: charity, courage, kindness, and all kinds of virtues that are lovely. If we have forgotten why the whole Christian story is so crowded with glory, it might just be that it promises through the grace and mercy of Jesus that every person can also be given a sense and a meaning that will outlast his or her days. Furthermore, this new life is the very stuff of life everlasting.

CHAPTER TWO

MAKING SENSE EMOTIONALLY

I

Emotions are usually described as something we suffer. They come upon us in circumstances that are often unpleasant. Anger is like that; therefore, we often say that we were overcome with rage or that suddenly a fit of anger came upon us. Some emotions are violent and are accompanied by physiological changes. With fear, we break out in a sweat, we feel faint, we become pale. With anger, we feel hot all over, we become flushed, our blood pressure rises. Because emotions like these are often vivid and pronounced, they truly become states we suffer. We seem passive. Sometimes we let emotions like these set the pattern for what all emotions are supposed to be—physical, dramatic, and mostly irrational. But other emotions, some with related names, are quite different. If you are afraid of heights, you may never blanch, and surely you are not prone to lash out at anything. Not all fears are debilitating, nor are all kinds of anger desperate.

An emotion like the fear of heights can be very powerful, but in a strikingly different way. You may never look afraid, but the chances are that you will never accept a doctor's appointment on the sixteenth floor, take trips through the mountains, or be quick about repairing your roof. In short, a large swath of your behavior is attributable to such an emotion, but nothing very spectacular characterizes your behavior. You do not typically suffer "states," but you do make allowances for yourself that most people without this fear would never do.

A fear, for example, that you might have because of great danger is probably justified. To know great peril is to fear, and someone who does not fear in such circumstances is irrational. A raging fire is fearful; so is a broken power line twisting amid spectators or an airliner that suddenly drops five thousand feet. Hence we can make a distinction. There are all kinds of emotions that belong to our general learning. Some of them are necessary components in the judgments we make about the world. They belong to our maturity and to our serious experience of everyday life. But other emotions get a grip on us, not on the world. They master us and sometimes distort and twist our ability to see affairs properly. These emotions do not help us make sense at all. They are more like clues to our own oddness than tokens of how the world is.

Thus far we have seen that emotions are very complex. They are a good part of what makes people so interesting and also so difficult to understand. No wonder, then, that emotions are variously described. On the one side, we can slip into saying that they are irrational, that they need to be controlled, and that they are often opposed to considered judgment. But we can just as easily agree that being without emotions is worse than being physically blind, that someone who is incapable of jealousy probably is bereft of real love, that to be without shame or the possibility of shame is to be a renegade. In fact, if you are not afraid of anything at all, you are downright foolish.

More particularly, we are going to try to show that by acquiring certain emotions we can also constitute ourselves as able and substantial persons. Already we have alluded to the fact that having no emotions or having the wrong ones can keep us unhappy and deprive us of satisfaction and sense. But the cure for that is not an emotionless and dispassionate life, despite what some austere rationalists have said; rather, we need the nurture, Christian nurture included, that will reduce our vulnerability to silly emotions and give us the strength to contend with our problems. Emotions will be described anew in this chapter, as we try to place them in context, to see how they are to be achieved, governed, corrected, and nurtured and how some new ones can actually be acquired. That Christianity helps us make sense of our lives by giving us a new set of emotions, even a new pathos, will be a good part of our theme.

II

A feeling is not the same as an emotion. To say this supposes a guarded use of the word "feeling." We do use it for a variety of purposes. When I ask, "How do you feel?", I'm not asking you about specific feelings or sensations. Here I want to know about your general well-being: how, as we say, you are judging yourself and your prospects. Feeling something to be smooth is like finding it to be so. So the word "feeling" has all kinds of uses. Usually we do not get confused, because the contexts are so different that the same word's different roles are not a problem. But there is a more particular use of the word "feeling." When I have a pain, I tell you how much it hurts. You have a right to ask me where I hurt; for if I have a pain, I have it somewhere. So, too, with a tickle, an itch, an ache; with nausea, thirst, hunger pangs, and the sensation of heat. We do not usually improve our itches, pains, and pangs—we simply have them, and usually in a certain place.

Furthermore, feelings come and go, usually as interruptions that demand our attention. They have duration, and we can time them if we choose. They can be there for a while, disappear completely, then reappear with a vengeance. If you enjoy having warm breezes envelop you as you sit in the sun, then you know how diffuse and general some pleasant feelings can be. Still, even the diffuseness is not enough to call your experience an emotion. Many emotions do not come with sensations; at any rate, we can have an emotion like hope, expectation, grief, jealousy, disappointment, or anxiety without sensations in any part making up the emotion. Sensations may accompany an emotion, as feeling faint sometimes accompanies a severe fear, but they do not constitute it.

Emotions, however, are quite different, at least if we stick with the very clear cases. Characteristic of hate is the fact that one has no increased respiration, no shaking, no peculiar sensations. Instead, hate is directed toward something or, perhaps more often, toward someone. Hate requires an object. It is transitive; it is aimed at something or someone. This is why emotions are all tied up with prepositions in our everyday language. We are disappointed "in" or "about" something; we are in love "with" that person; we are angry "at," perturbed "about," jealous "toward," or saddened "by" states of affairs, events, or persons. But typically, the logic of an emotion is to answer the question "About what?" whereas the logic of a feeling is to answer to the question "Where?" Emotions are different from feelings, too, in being affects that we have some responsibility for. They are corrigible in certain ways. One can stop fearing, refrain from hoping, decide not to be jealous, and certainly get over grief. Likewise, there is little sense in asking "where" one hopes or fears, for hoping and fearing are not located somewhere as feelings are.

Furthermore, feelings come and go in a different way than emotions do. I cannot stop pain or start it quite the way I can stop or start fearing. Here we have to think about examples. With an emotion I often have to change the way I am thinking before the emotion changes. It does not go away like an itch does. Grief is assuaged by the passage of time, and finding another interest to take up one's time will often help. We can lose hope, but usually because we now live differently or have concluded something radically at variance with what we formerly believed. Emotions are vulnerable to the way we evaluate the world around us, and they change as deliberately or as nondeliberately as our general conceptions of daily existence. Feelings, on the other hand, are radically independent of such matters. We suffer nausea, hunger, pain, and fatigue under rather specific physical conditions, but not very often because of the way we evaluate those conditions.

Also, we do suffer moods. Sometimes we get confused by the various words we have for what were once called "affects." In living a human life we are variously affected, i.e., changes and effects are noticeable in our subjective life. So we are touched, stirred, and influenced, and then we develop all kinds of richly differentiated ways of responding. We are variously acted upon by our own history, by other people, and by the conditions around us. We hope, fear, love, and so on in conjunction with, and often as a part of, understanding, liking, caring, and knowing. That is a way of describing one sort of "affect," our emotions. But then we are also capable of moods. The reason for the category of "moods" is clear enough as soon as we think of the range of "affects" we call moods. Irritability is one, melancholy another. Still other, different moods are despondency, anxiety, despair, a certain kind of guilt, and even petulance and argumentativeness. These have something in common that makes us call them "moods" rather than emotions or feelings.

For one thing, moods take in everything. If someone asks you what you are despondent about, you can say, "Nothing in particular, but everything in general." This is the way it is, too, with petulance, irritability, and anxiety. A mood has no target; or, it is as if everything, and hence no single thing, is its target. Therefore, moods do not change with things in the world, nor are they governed by the character of events or people we meet with from day to day. If you are pessimistic, that means "you" are that way no matter how the world is. Optimism is, most of the time, a mood, and it can sometimes be quite absurd, especially if there is no reason for it. There are moods that are pleasant and moods that are not. For example, cheerfulness is a mood. Sometimes we do not quite know what makes us so buoyant and ebullient—nothing seems to make any difference. Certainly we would like to be like that always, for then we would have an easy equanimity, a kind of satisfaction, and even confidence. But then our mood changes. Everything then looks dark and gloomy. Both extremes, cheerfulness and gloom, are, typically, moods. Both are often irrational, too.

This marks another characteristic of human moodiness. Some of us are continually vulnerable to shifts like this, from highs to lows, from confidence to anxiety, hope to despair, elation to gloom. Surely this is a big part of everyone's psychological history. Once more, there have been all kinds of theories proposed to give an account of these forms of desperation and unhappiness. We cannot deny the extreme cases when physical causes are responsible or when something unconscious may be triggering the vacillation. But we are altogether too quick to give the task of making sense of our lives to others when there are personal resources already at hand. The fact is that most genuine emotions are tolerable, especially when we also know their genesis and justification. The difficulty arises when emotions are fed from within, from our own life and history; then they frequently turn into powerful and irrational moods. A specific fear can easily be magnified into an anxiety about everything at once. Anger over a minor slight can become a generalized resentment over differences of status and vocation for which no one has any responsibility. A disappointment about a small failure can convert into large-scale despair about the future of humankind.

Moods, after a bit of living and self-cultivation, become symptoms of the person, even though they usually are articulated as judgments about the world and others. Moods often deceive those of us who suffer them. We become accomplices to the mood; soon thinking is affected and we can no longer trust our own judgments. The anxious person finds troubles where there are none; the melancholic individual sees nothing to be glad about, no matter where he or she looks; and if dread gets us in its grip, the awfulness of circumstances will be inevitable. Surely, the person here is the source of the dismaying "affects," not of the way the world or people are. It is the individual, not the world, that does not make sense. Moods are like that. They make us incapable of forming true judgments and liable to a range of pathos that is often inappropriate.

Moods, emotions, and feelings have been mentioned, but there are more so-called affects. We have many other words in our vocabulary that are perhaps not clear to us. We talk about attitudes, sentiments, and passions. Sometimes these words are used loosely to cover a wide array of affects, as when we say, "He is very passionate," and mean only that he is interesting because of his wide range of emotions and moods. Unfortunately, the word "passionate" sometimes conveys only the thought of sexual promiscuity, but that use is too narrow for our present subject. Instead, we will use "passion" to describe a long-term affect, something that looks like an emotion, but with one large difference. A passion is usually long in duration, yet it too is directed toward an object. A person who collects postage stamps can be said to have a passion for them when he or she persists in buying them, gives up other interests for the sake of them, and does this for a lifetime. Ordinary emotions about stamps are not obvious anymore. The surprises are few, the glee is muted, the enthusiasm is not vocal; instead, the passion is evinced by more subtle kinds of behavior, more pronounced habits, and a steely determination to get more stamps. To speak of a "passion" here can account for a great deal of behavior and still be without any particular instances of emotion. Some great lovers are like that, too, when they no longer evince the wild array of emotions but, instead, are faithful and considerate for a lifetime.

Some people, to their credit, are said to have a passion for justice. One has to think carefully about how and where a person would be qualified to be so described, which certainly would not include easy talk about equity and the ordinary array of emotions over something one liked. No, a passion is more comprehensive than an emotion or even a group of emotions. We would distrust a person who displayed emotion about instances of inequality, who sighed with anguish and grew faint with horror but then showed nothing more. It takes comparatively little to be easily moved to tears or laughter, but it takes a great passion to do something specific about human suffering and folly.

There are reasons for this. Marital love, for example, is supposed to be a passion. It is not an enthusiasm of the moment, not mere elation, not just a pang of love; it is not even like being generally appreciative or widely affectionate; instead, it is love that is held in place by a promise, by obligations, by vows, and by a host of decisions. One certainly knows instances when such marital love produces a host of emotions, all kinds of immediate joys and pleasures, and a plethora of feelings. But the passion itself is less immediate and more a matter of an acquired way of responding. One does not "fall" into passions like marital love or even patriotism. Someone who cares deeply about one's country does not have to like everything or approve of every policy. Patriotism is compatible with criticism, wrongdoing, and disappointments. You need not waver with every adversity or search out some immutables before you give your nation your allegiance. Being patriotic describes an acquired proneness to be loyal in a variety of circumstances. However, such a passion is surely the very seed ground in which emotions are apt to grow and others very likely to die. Passions are like that. They bespeak the large-scale, more widely conceived dispositions that we can bring to fruition in our daily lives.

Passions are less immediate in another way. We do not expect deep hatred from a child; dislike, yes, but hatred, no. For hatred—as over against a passing dislike—is a passion too. It involves perhaps some experience, some reflection, maybe a few decisions. In consequence, we hold people responsible for their passions because we think they represent a history in which and for which a certain responsibility has been gained. Therefore, patriotism is often to a person's credit, just as marital love is. Such passions organize a person in a vivid way. They are not symbolic of the person; instead, they are the means of making the self and the person. Here, then, passions show still another difference from emotions, from feelings, and certainly, as we shall note, from sentiments.

Like emotions, passions are directed at something. But sentiments are somewhat different from both. Of course, we have to recognize the very wide and somewhat diffuse use of that term, too, but we are not using it in a general way. Instead, we note the more particularized usage: for example, when we speak of a person being only "sentimental" and not quite mature. Here we have another, yet familiar, use. Then we think of persons who have sentiments, but who have them almost as affectations and artifices. Someone is sentimental who talks love with other persons, sheds a tear or two, but never does anything to share an interest or bear the others' tasks. Or in another way, a sentiment is an emotion that does not consider the objective situations that are appropriate. Consider the person who is effete—who enjoys tears, who sighs sweetly about the pain of others, or who speaks resoundingly of defending the country without lifting a finger. This person indulges aspects of the emotions and passions without accepting the facts, the responsibilities, and the duties that also belong with them. This is what makes for what we call sentiments.

Sentimentality can easily characterize people who are esthetically inclined. If one indulges in literature endlessly, if one enjoys art and artifacts, if one contemplates ideas and simply likes them, then one can easily make an indulgent vocation of merely entertaining thoughts and forms of pathos. Soon one's whole life becomes like a substitute, a pale replica of what it ought to be. One duplicates in oneself only that part of the passion or the emotion that one finds in the artifacts and lives of others. This can happen, also, to the readers of such taxing literature as that of Tolstoy, or Augustine, or Flannery O'Connor, or Dostoevsky. Soon one is sighing, grieving, being moved to indignation, but only on paper or as one reads. However sophisticated this may all seem and however long it may take to get this way, one may still stay a sentimental and shallow person through it all. If one has rich responses only when reading a book or remembering David Copperfield, and very paltry responses to the hurts and tribulations of one's own life and that of others, then one is, very likely, only mawkishly tender, a sentimentalist.

Making sense of one's own emotions is quite different from responding to those of another person, especially a fictional character. But more, a sentimental person has learned the behavior associated with an emotion—the crying, the pity, the woeful sighs—and enjoys all of that. Augustine talks about his unhappy days of miserable delirium, when he enjoyed even the pangs of sorrow—not least in the theater. He continues: "I always looked for things to wring my heart, and the more tears an actor caused me to shed by his performance on the stage, even though he was portraying the imaginary distress of others, the more delightful and attractive I found it." (Augustine, *Confessions,* tr. with an Introduction by R. S. Pine-Coffin, pp. 56–57; Penguin Books, 1961.)

The emotional chaos in which he lived made him zealous for more and more artificial stimulants to his emotional life, for he was incapable of deep charity or any gripping pathos. "Could the life I led be called true life?" he asks.

Though this is an extreme case, sentimentality has this kind of logic. A sentimentalist yields to the need for emotional gratification but does it by carefully selecting the circumstances. Instead of experiencing real emotions that forge a new consciousness and toughen up one's mode of taking in the world, the sentimentalist forges an artificial and shallow synthesis.

Perhaps something should be said here about attitudes. But we will forego that topic and return to it later in another context. Nonetheless, we have noted thus far a variety of ways that are already named for us in our common diction. We have distinguished emotions, feelings, passions, sentiments, and moods. This has been done chiefly to make more plausible and understandable our subsequent remarks about how we can overcome the emotional and moody chaos we frequently suffer. We are also moving in the direction of seeing what is involved in having a new life made for us in Christ Jesus.

III

Some indices of a life that does not make sense are a perpetual restlessness, a gnawing anxiety, and even despair. But these are not all. Perhaps a more succinct way to characterize the person, maybe oneself, who is no longer coping with the business of living is to say that one is not content. A kind of sickness of spirit ensues, and living hardly seems worthwhile. In short, one is unhappy. Besides, the very capacities for happiness seem to dry up, and hence the prospects for well-being get more and more circumscribed. Obviously, all kinds of causes may be at work in some cases, and my remarks here are not intended to cover all instances of wretchedness. Those to which we will allude are marked by emotional distress, often a consequence of either negative and intrinsically hurtful emotions, or a kind of emotional life that has allowed moods to dominate all prospects and judgments.

Let us note a few examples. Most of us live with sets of circumstances that will sooner or later disappoint us. We seldom are masters of very much of the domain in which we live. It is not long before we develop expectations about ourselves, about the prospects that are suggested to us, and begin to revel in the promise of the future. All this may be done with thoughtfulness and with due regard for the fund of experience of oneself and others. Soon one may develop hope, or hopes. "Hope" is an affect too, one of the ways to make use of the future as we see it. But if you live with a thought for that future, you also become liable to an exquisite kind of dismay. The world may not work out as you had hoped, and your self-evaluation may be shattered by your unexpected weaknesses and even failures. All this may be private to you. Perhaps only you suffer both the aspiration and the disappointment.

However, there is something right about hoping itself. Someone who does not hope probably has no vision of the morrow, perhaps no plans and no purposes. Hopes belong to the very texture of thinking, especially thinking about the future that all of us face. Hence, hoping is not a hobby of some people, and certainly it is not just a luxury for those who have leisure. The very character of a human mode of life requires it. Furthermore, we mature into hope; someone who has never learned to hope would be a failure as a person. We cannot quite imagine what it would be like to be without hope. Correlatively, to have lost all hope is the prelude to deep meaninglessness. To gain hope again, after a long loss of expectancy and zeal, marks the return of vitality and life.

This is why the animal cannot be credited with hopes. The

dog may salivate over the prospect of food, but that is part of an expectation, not quite a hope. And the infant does a lot of interesting things, but it typically does not hope. In fact, hoping comes rather late in a life history. It is not a skill at all, and it surely is not quite what one can call an action or an activity. This, too, may seem strange, for we do have an active verb, "hoping," which suggests that we are doing something when we hope. Likewise, "not hoping" portends a loss of something, or a failure to behave in a certain fashion. An example might be useful. If a child's father came home from work and heard the mother say, "You won't believe it, but I caught Johnny hoping today!" the father ought to be surprised. After all, Johnny takes his first step, he learns his name, he says a few words, and he counts. You can catch him in all these actions. But hoping would not be one of them. Yet he does learn to do it, sometime later.

This is also the way it is with other elaborate and many-sided emotions. Clearly, emotions are never precise and isolable bits of behavior. They belong in the texture of a very complicated form of life that only mature persons can achieve. Some emotions, like gratitude and awe, seem never to develop at all among some people. Emotions are not acts, not episodes, but ways that people learn to respond to a very complex and puzzling world. Certainly, one can assert that hoping is not quite an ability, though there are those who hope significantly and there are those who fail. Hoping is not quite a skill, though a lifetime may be necessary to learn how to do it. What then is hope? If it belongs anywhere, it probably belongs among what we can call capacities. For I also learn a certain capaciousness; I make room in my life for it. Hope is an acquired capacity, one that develops as soon as I learn to cope with a future, plan for a career, and anticipate consequences for my actions. Again, my dog, my infant child—and those who refuse to form their lives at all—typically have no hope.

Surely, we learn to hope. In a strange way, though, in acquiring capacities like the emotions, we have examples to follow but not, strictly speaking, teachers. Many people can be taught to play the piano, because a variety of skills are needed, and each can be learned, one by one, from a teacher. Esthetic taste, for example, is not quite like that. This rare capacity is learned, but in a wide number of circumstances and over a period of time. Like an emotion, it cannot be stopped the way a skill can be, nor is it marked by a single exercise or achievement. A whole person, on the other hand, becomes tasteful, sensitive, and discriminating, and it is not the fingers, thoughts, or eyes alone that are trained, though all may exemplify the taste. So it is, too, with hope. Gradually, most of us so live that hope has a place, and a large place, in our lives. It is one of the ways we are formed into persons. Yet it is also one of the points at which we are most susceptible to chaos and the breakup of our very mode of life.

Certainly the grammar of life itself elicits from all of us some kinds of hope. We live with a modicum of decency and endurance if we keep some hopes alive. Without hope we soon find life itself unbearable. However, a loss of hope does not happen all at once. Hope usually builds up slowly as we assess ourselves, the world around us, and the particularities of our situation. Safe to say, most of us are rather crude empiricists in this matter, letting the flux and flow of events suggest the possibilities. But then two major flaws begin to develop. A certain number of people find that with disappointments in ourselves and in our social and economic prospects, and with the odd and fortuitous way the world works out, it is indeed easy to trim down one's hopes. The same world that elicits our expectations can also thwart them. Who among us has not had to fight the deepest disappointments? When some of us think back on the way we wanted to forge our marriage in the crucibles of love and courage, and then when we see how paltry our accomplishments are in this respect, we are prone to think that hoping itself is vanity.

Sometimes the frustration of our hopes and the agonies we suffer when nothing seems to work out can lead us to disparage hoping altogether. This often is how hopes are lost. They wither away under the stress of daily life. Frequently, hopes are replaced by a kind of cynicism about ourselves or an active disparagement of human possibilities. But hope stays an emotion if we keep a prospect in view, and disappointment stays a manageable emotion if we keep our thoughts pointed to the way things actually are. Thus far, human affairs remain tractable. But we can make all this bigger and worse. We can slip into large-scale despair about the world, and more especially about ourselves. Sometimes we have a right to feel despair (as an emotion) if, for example, we see how helpless the promises really are that are made by utopian political dreamers about human prospects. Everybody who has tasted war certainly hopes—indeed, longs—for peace among nations. If anyone is misled by the prospect of world government, or a "Pax Romana," or democratization of all nations, that person is surely entitled to despair about such grandiose talk. Some of the despair over planning, over communism, over socialism, over international law and other proposals made into nostrums for all social evils is richly deserved. Despair here, provided that it is targeted, is legitimate and belongs to a sage and detailed assessment of how the world actually works.

This kind of despair is indeed an emotion, and it can be the very means of correcting our hopes and refounding them on a better assessment of the way the world is. With this, however hurtful, we can have no serious quarrel. But despair is such an easy emotion for mature people to nurture. Live a little longer, think a little harder, we like to believe, and hope springs up. Before one has tried one's own powers and tasted the world's resistance, hope too is very easy. This must have been why a poet said that hope springs eter-

nal in the human breast. Live a little longer, and despair also
prospers. One kind we have already noted; it has its justification. But there is another kind that feeds on the consciousness of our own inadequacies and weaknesses. The result of this is that the despair may start as an assessment of
oneself, but it will transmute into a moody assessment of
one's entire prospect, one's whole future, eventually the
whole of human life. Despair often begins with the fractur-
ing of one's hopes—by accidents, by mistakes, by failures, by
circumstances like poverty, joblessness, ill health, and great
sorrows. Hardly anyone is prepared for all that happens in a
lifetime, and surely we cannot predict our own strengths
when we so seldom meet the same thing twice.

Sometimes we are bold enough to suppose that the world
can be engineered to make it safe against catastrophe, death,
and mishaps. In the middle of the awesome difficulty of coping with the terrifying way that cancer strikes us, or infla-
tion corrodes our savings, or international conflicts invade
even our homes—amid all that, there are still those who en-
vision the new role of science, or the rise of a new econom-
ics, and who foresee surcease from all this for posterity.

Earlier, we noted how two fundamental flaws in our emotional life can begin to take shape. One we have just mentioned, namely, the despair that takes root as our hopes are
vanquished. Once despair lives in us, the whole world begins to look dark. The air of desperation that is fostered in
ourselves keeps everything gloomy. Not even the little successes and small virtues of daily life give any consolation. We
will note more of this form of the human personality later.
Here we turn to another major breakdown that our emotions can help produce.

The other fundamental flaw keeps up the facade of hope,
and hence of happiness, by a different ploy altogether.
Surely some of us know this for ourselves. We can let hopes
go on and on, and they multiply and get so comprehensive
that it is almost as if reality slips away from us. Some people

develop a dream world, one of the imagination, that causes them not to respond to the realities around them. Surely there is real desperation at the root of those views which say there is no sickness and no evil. A kind of metaphysics that says the world around us is an illusion can be fed by the desperate need to have reality accord with our hopes. When the everyday world gets intolerable, it is easy to construct another account of it. Far be it from me to argue that all views that deny the world around us are fed by this despairing motive or by the need for an objectivity that matches our need. But surely some of them are. For there is a silly side to human hoping, too. Who of us does not know someone who evades all fundamental change in his or her own personality by insisting, instead, that all he or she needs is a change in jobs and then everything will be better? Then a vain hope takes over. People change mates with utter abandon, always led by the hopeful thought that the difficulty is in the other person. Some hope for a life in the country when urban life is impossible; some indulge in fantasies about retirement being their golden years when they have refused to re-form themselves all through their working years. College teachers insist they cannot realize their potential until they are in the prestigious environment they have garnished with their hopes. Ministers preach badly because, so they say, they have never had a congregation equal to their abilities.

In cases like these, a host of misjudgments are made about situations, oneself, and the range of possibilities. One of the awful features of hopes that are never corrected is that they begin, instead, to grow anew and to change continually. Eventually they lead to a disparagement of reality itself. Whatever sense one begins to make then is at a terrible cost. It is as if the satisfaction and even happiness that we can have by staying hopeful is increasingly hollow. Soon other people begin to see the evasions, the excuses, and the self-justification, but often the individual who falsely hopes does not. A tragic note in all this is that when one continually hopes in this vain way, the grip on one's own reality, on oneself, is absent. So people, wanting to stay young, begin to act as if they are, letting hopes deny their years.

Certainly a deep vanity awaits all of us if our hopes are never tutored. Hoping that is undisciplined, that lets itself be fed by the fecundity of invention and the never-ending stream of possibilities that intelligence can conjure up, soon loses all sense of the fundamental distinction that marks meaningfulness for all of us, the distinction between the real and the unreal. Unreal hopes make the person who has them also unreal. And then one's life makes little or no sense. Earlier we noted that with the disappearance of hope and the increase of despair, with attendant anxiety, with dread of the future and a restlessness that has no surcease, living becomes burdensome and pointless. However, such despair usually intimates its presence; often, at least, a person is aware of being in some kind of difficulty. But with hopes that keep shifting and expanding, there is often little or no self-awareness. How silly a person looks who knows himself or herself so little that he or she never takes the measures to achieve success, all the while contemplating the raptures it will bring. Surely it is right to say that "the natural flights of the human mind are not from pleasure to pleasure, but from hope to hope" (Samuel Johnson in *The Rambler*, March 24, 1750).

Against all this there is something fundamental and plain to be said about Christian nurture. Unfortunately, the popular thought of our day has it that everything personal is a resignation of the highest task, a veritable concession to self-centeredness and something antiquated. Worse yet, religious leadership is prone to lump all such efforts toward personal nurture with conservative pessimism about change or with vulgar religious movements that are against liberation and social policy-making. But here we shall insist upon the contrary, namely, that the New Testament, as well as the Old, puts into our life stream that kind of teaching which will reconstitute us as people, individually and socially. This has been neglected by erstwhile conservatives as well as liberals, by Biblicists as well as modernists, sometimes out of embarrassment and incompetence with such intimate personal matters, and sometimes because of a mistaken view that human subjectivity is entirely whimsical and private anyway, quite out of reach of any teaching, either moral or Christian.

This we insist is both misleading and wrong. But our case will be made indirectly by showing that Christian teachings require new emotions as firmly and as clearly as they require new judgments and another view of life.

IV

It is a mistake to assume that emotions are standard, discrete, and easily identifiable. For example, all of us are familiar with the use of the word "fear." Yet sooner or later even that simple word comes to have many uses in naming and describing not just one kind of experience but a wide variety of experiences, states, and even convictions. The fact that the word is general has given credibility to the idea that there is a standard "fear," a kind of universal norm for the word. Such is not the case. Think, for example, of the teaching that "the fear of the Lord is the beginning of wisdom." At the outset we can see that this fear is not the paralyzing, cringing kind that makes it impossible to respond. The fear that a poisonous snake is in your sleeping bag might make you unable to move, even to cry out. But the fear of God is not like that.

Most of us apparently do not know God; otherwise, we would surely not be so casual, so nonchalant, even to the extent of using his name so carelessly. For the God of the Bible is not a chum, not just a chance acquaintance, not someone inviting easy familiarity. To know that God is to fear him. Without the fear of God, one could not be quite sure of correct knowledge of him. But a word is needed about that fear.

Certainly it is more like awe and regard, a kind of wariness, probably the sort that would mean watching your step in his presence.

Two aspects are discernible here. When God is characterized as worthy of fearful regard, one learns some theology, something about God. It would be very odd to be an expert on God without experiencing this fearful aspect. Those of us who are apt to ask for the objective teachings first, the plain teachings, without the emotional and subjective side, are easily misled here. It is not as if you can have objective teachings on one occasion and then, as a matter of preference, decide to be fearful on another occasion. Nor is the fear separable in quite that way. For to know that God is fearful is already to fear. Thus the teaching about God cannot be entertained correctly without fear's being part of the mode of assimilating the meaning. In fact, spinning the word "God" around on your tongue without the fear being there is just to indulge in a bit of nonsense.

This shows that the cultivation of the emotions is an intimate part of the Christian teachings. Not all this teaching can be done in a single hour, or in one book, or only in the sermon and liturgy. Nonetheless, no one who purports to be a Christian teacher can neglect the emotions, for they are an essential part of the very texture of the teachings themselves. This is to note something else, too: that the close connections between the verbal teachings—the doctrines, beliefs, stories, and judgments involving God—and the emotional life of persons means that a learner's access may be by means of either. Sometimes we have heard Christians say things about love, fear, or hope, probably when it looked as if they were only foundering emotionally. However, Christian nurture requires that these emotions be governed, produced, and ordered according to what God is and how he is related to the world. Therefore, those emotions, if they be Christianly conceived, will probably tug us also into belief in God, Jesus, and God's creation and sustaining of the world.

Teaching might sometimes start with those attractive emotions being offered to us, at least in crucial situations in daily life. But the beliefs must follow. Likewise, the teachings and the beliefs about Christian objectivities will certainly, if done right, elicit a new pattern of emotions, which is also mandatory. One cannot properly have one without the other.

This might sound fantastic and quite impossible if it were not for one further consideration. It is not as if all this has to be done to us. As suggested earlier, we can easily turn Christianity into sentiments, especially about love, fellowship, and all of humankind. But sentiments are emotions without full content and orientation to things as they are. Christianity is not a matter of toying with our emotional capacities apart from the cultivation of thoughtfulness. On the contrary, it is in understanding a variety of teachings that the emotions are also enjoined. There is a reciprocity, too, for in the acknowledgment of the deep emotional needs for peace, hope, and the cessation of shame, the teachings also come into focus. A few more particular cases might help us see that.

If we live in continual dread of the future, that dread casts out any prospect of happiness. Dread, a dark kind of mood, is a "mood" precisely because it has lost most resemblance to the fears that one might have started with. We might fear the surgery that is pending on the morrow, or we might fear meeting an adversary or critic during the next month. But dread comes about when the entire future is gathered up and made portentous. Then we dread reminders of the future as well as the future itself, and nothing can assuage our dread of the prospects. This is also what happens when we are fearful of being found out, when we shudder over the thought of someone knowing how we really are. Friends become threatening, and every question is like a weapon being used against us.

So it is, too, with anxiety, especially the kind that floats from one thing to another. This helpless kind of nervousness that feeds on what "might happen" can take root very easily, all the more so when we are gifted in entertaining all the possibilities. Strangely, such an anxiety is not helped much by the advice to stop and think. That usually is why a person is so anxious, because he or she cannot stop thinking. Both dread and anxiety are sustained by thinking, and both cause human life to lose its point. We have to remember that we do not have emotions and then remain the same; moods especially, but emotions too, mark ways that we change. "We" become hopeless, desperate, wretched, ashamed, and unhappy. Our moods and these frightening negative emotions become modifiers of our persons. This is why we suffer so and why our suffering makes living so burdensome.

Yet this is also why Christian teachings are said to be glad tidings. It is not only that they might interest a reader for their romancing charm or suggest alternatives to the philosopher's speculation. They are gladsome, too, because they offer an altogether new set of emotions: genuine emotions, with objects and actual states of affairs brought back into view. For example, against the ordinary view of the world, where change seems to be king and where continual adaptation and apprehensive shifts of attitudes are expected, we are asked to think about God, who is eternal and an everlasting goodness. It is exceedingly difficult to think about such a God and then stay restless. For he is not always moving, and in him is something lasting and always worthy. To have one's mind fixed on him is a worthy purpose only if one's mind can then become less anxious. The weather can be thought about at length, but the weather is not thereby changed. If you are cold, you do not become warm by thinking about how cold it is. Being cold is to suffer a feeling. Being anxious is a little different. When we add God to our picture of the world, the world becomes altogether different. If we learn that he has it in his care, that he mixes concern with providential love, then the shortness of our lives, the transitoriness of knowledge, the vanity of rulers—everything that produces anxiety—also takes on another aspect. To think that way is to come to rest. What chance does anxiety or dread have when the world is redescribed as God's?

This is why moods like anxiety and dread do not have great survival value. Think about them; how absurd they are as human postures in God's world! The new life in Christ Jesus is simply daring an occasion to view the world from above, almost as God would have it in his view. We have to be careful here, of course. If we think of events in the perspective of a hundred years, nothing seems important. We call this the Stoic way, and it is a familiar therapy under a thousand guises. But this way dispels all emotion and solves problems by suggesting that we need not be affected at all. Christianity does not propose quite that. With the Christian perspective comes the dispersal of the old moods. It is almost as if now we can exult in confidence and hope, instead. The moods of anxiety, dread, and maybe even despair can be corrected and disciplined by putting everything—insofar as this is plausible—before a loving God and Father, who cares for all that is.

The new aspect, absent from most perspectival views, is that we are still entitled to genuine emotions. We do not have to fear the morrow in that unwholesome, restless way. We are now living in relation to a God who is our author and our sustainer. Furthermore, he makes it all add up, and all we can do is to cooperate. Our point, then, is that a stream of new emotional health is awaiting us.

No longer are we entitled to despair. Those of us who think the world is tragic because of afflictions, accidents, and deep frustrations are forced by the Christian teaching to a new level of consciousness. Indeed, whether the world is tragic or heavenly is not ours to conclude—that is God's affair. But this is something not to be told by the fortunate to the unfortunate but by one sufferer to another. Christianity is not a way out of the numerous hazards and pains of daily living as much as it is a way of meeting them. Too often we want to use prayer and even God to lessen the calamities, and then we make our faith a means to an end. Before we ask that much, we are bound to the task of meeting whatever befalls us with the armor of God, and this includes love, hope, and a powerful sense of the worthwhileness of a life lived under his tutelage.

How can we despair if we remember that God made us and loves us? How can we not have hope when the prospect is eternal life, the cessation of all sorrows, and a kind of blessedness? Such hope is not just talk, and it is not significantly evinced even by doctrines about hope. Too often we seem to think that the religious life can be essayed by reading, by getting the Bible straight, by discussion, and then by indulging in a kind of religious talkativeness in the presence of others. All this can go on while we suffer in the poverty of genuine emotions! If anyone suffers despair, the chances are very good that the despair is noticeable. Not always, but usually. For despair means that you lack enthusiasm, that few discriminations any longer mark a significant difference, that nothing much matters. Soon motivation disappears and one does not care to act at all. Indeed, despair then becomes noticeable. We would find it odd to say that despair is articulated chiefly in a point of view or in endless talk, though assuredly that too can occur. Instead, despair is read off as behavior if it is manifested to us at all.

Certainly, hope is like that too. We do not have hope chiefly as a point of view. Christ Jesus is the Christian hope, but this is only to say that he is the object and even the cause for the Christian's hope. If one has a new hope in Christ Jesus, then this, too, is portrayed like most deep emotions are, in the large number of ways we are affected. In learning to hope, we also discuss an unending source of motivations that are not easily frustrated and not vanquished by local defeats. That is what one might expect of a hope rooted in God

Almighty, in contrast to a hope in a cause, a program, or other persons. But I have to discover that source of motivation, and only in that can I dismiss genuine despair. Also, to have hope is to be hopeful, and that means to be zealous and enthusiastic about one's tasks. Again, the sign of the hope may be that one talks hopefully, but a more powerful symptom would surely be that one lives with zeal and purpose.

All this is a reminder that Christian teaching is many-sided, probably because it is addressed to persons whom God seems to have made that way. The Christian teacher, along with the church and its various modes of addressing people, must be aware of this God-given potential that each of us has.

CHAPTER THREE

MAKING SENSE MORALLY

I

One of the uncomfortable facts about ourselves is that we all must live in a way that meets our own approval. A bad conscience is the awareness that we have not behaved as we should. The longer and more thoughtfully we live, the deeper such a view of ourselves becomes. Soon we no longer think only of this or that lapse or decision or deed that was wrong, we begin to evaluate ourselves as a kind of totality. The whole person comes into perspective, and we begin to regret what we have made of ourselves. We do not easily entertain our intentions, our motives, or our purposes, because after a while these too look ambiguous, unclear, and sometimes even wild. We want to do what we ought, but we also want to enjoy ourselves; we seek the good in the situation, but we also want to please everybody; we strive to serve God, but we surely never forget what we deserve from Mammon. When all this happens, our life becomes blurred again, and we can hardly bear the light of our own thought upon it. Furthermore, we become secretly wretched, our conscience gives us no peace, and the tasks of living get burdensome.

It does little good, then, to heed the advice that comes so

easily: "Don't think so much about yourself!" "Get busy!" "Take it easy!" "Have a nice day!" We would like to oblige, but these suggestions do not seem adequate for what ails us. For we are beginning to discover the plain truth, that we are moral beings. We also have to make sense with our deeds and behavior, with our purposes, motives, and accomplishments. In a peculiar yet very detailed way, most of us discover that we are judges of ourselves, that we project ideals for ourselves, that we are accountable not only to others but to ourselves as well. Instead of not thinking about ourselves and not having self-concern, it seems necessary, rather, to have a great deal of concern and to be very thoughtful about what one is making of oneself.

Certainly all of us are sooner or later in this kind of situation. When we were very young, someone else took care of us, even deciding what we should do and when. But with maturity, that begins to change. We suddenly discover that we are responsible for our own existence, not only physically but morally. Now we have to decide whether we are going to be honest, courageous, temperate, lazy, and clean, and also godly. Eventually there is no one but oneself to depend on in these matters.

Before too long we all are cognizant of the fact that we do have to live a life of which we can approve. It is not enough merely to please others, for groups, societies, churches, and even families change, and they do not always speak with a common voice. Furthermore, in growing up most of us want desperately to be ourselves and not to be only what others will make of us. Everybody remembers a bit of rebellion, perhaps, when one wanted thoughts of one's own, a slant that was distinctive, some freedom to decide, and, surely, the liberty to explore all kinds of behavior. Rules and duties, expectations and laws, commands and what others wanted—all felt oppressive and onerous. Everybody seemed willing to tell us what was right, but we began to resent always being told what was right. We wanted to discover even that for ourselves.

No one is quite so bold as to think that one can afford to be in the wrong or to live preferring what is evil. Human rebellion never goes quite that far. What we protest is the fact that others, the society, the church, and our elders, decide what is right for us. Here we would like to be competent ourselves, make decisions, and bear the responsibility—so, at least, we say. What makes all this so momentous is that our daily happiness and the very worth of our lives is at stake. This is why both sides feel the issues so deeply: parents and legislators of human affairs know all too well where human waywardness can lead, and the young surmise all too quickly what dull compliance and conformity can do to their lives. Both want the right and the good, and in ways that often conflict.

The Bible speaks to this situation in almost a matter-of-fact way when it worries its readers about the need for justification. There is not much of an argument presented for that notion; instead, the common human situation of discovering that one requires a life that is right and righteous, that is happy and justifiable, is simply assumed. Surely this theme from both the Old and the New Testament has to do with the conception that a life can be invalid and simply not worth much of anything. On the other hand, it proposes always that every life can also become valid and that its worth can be saved and established. Two appropriate factors can be noted here. One is that the Bible would not speak to the human condition at all if it were not that each person can discover for himself or herself this need for rightness. The Bible addresses a state of affairs for each person that threatens to break down, that is full of potential for disaster. It is made for seekers, for sojourners, for those who need justification and validity. And part of its content is plainly moral, telling us how laws and commands can meet the indigence of the human spirit. This acknowledgment of the human factor, the plain truth that each of us knows about himself or herself, is a constant factor, bridging the Bible and the everyday world we all know. All this, then, is the first of the two factors we want to note.

The other factor is a little more difficult to understand. The Bible, in contrast to perhaps our own unaided reflection and that of most moral teachers in history, also puts this whole business of the need for justification in a radically different perspective. It conceives of us all in the presence of a living God who is not just powerful and terrifying but also holy and good. Furthermore, this Bible dares to say that God's chief interest is not only the cosmos at large and the machinery of the universe but also the justification and validation, the saving, of humankind. What becomes my concern when I become most sensitive to myself and most intelligent about my prospects—namely, my prospects for rightness—is also God's interest in making the world, in manifesting himself in Jesus Christ, and in giving us access to grace and mercy. In a bold and declaratory fashion, the Bible asserts that while God is our maker and our judge, he is also our very justification and vindication.

This second factor brings us to the heart of both Testaments, not least to the story of Jesus' birth, life, death, and resurrection, all of which combine to make possible a forgiven and utterly grace-filled life. We have already alluded to the notion that this new life engendered in us by the life of Jesus can be lived zestfully, even hopefully, lovingly, and happily. Some very powerful emotions can now replace the anxiety, dread, disappointment, and even despair that most of us otherwise succumb to in living a natural and civil life. We earlier asserted that a new kind of emotional sense was ours once we dared to live the Christian life.

There is something like that available for us morally, also. Hence, we will now note how the acquisition of virtues will help bring some order and even a certain kind of style into our everyday living.

II

The notion of the "virtues" probably makes us think of something desiccated, prim, and uninteresting. For a variety of reasons, including some theological and religious ones, the very idea of a virtue has gone out of fashion. For example, recent popular notions about morality have been in the direction of thinking about self-expression, self-development, and, above all, about each person developing his or her own individuality in creative and pleasurable ways. That it cannot be wrong if it feels so good, looks so good, and, besides, if everybody is doing it—all these notions loom up as the modern style of living and thinking. But such notions are not actually modern at all, nor are they a peculiar feature of our scientific culture, our permissiveness, and the new freedoms. Instead, every person has had, and still has, the raw material, the flesh-and-blood impulses and pleasure drives, to act and to think in such ways. These ways are as old and as natural and, furthermore, as easy as any practices and beliefs that have ever been articulated. They do not arise because of the way societies and cultures are; rather, they arise because people are initially prone to doing their own thing and seeking immediate satisfactions before all else. People are and have been that way from the beginning of recorded time.

It is just this state of affairs that called forth the virtues in the first place and has made them look like the rational and sensible way to meet the needs of both our natural life and our social living. If everyone does his or her own thing, then it is very hard for the untalented, the poor, and the little ones of the world. Besides, if each does his or her own thing, so much depends upon health, youth, personal appetites, and all kinds of other accidental components of one's life. Very few of these stay constant, and a mode of life dependent upon them often has to be almost whimsical, momentary, and even inconstant just to stay appropriate. So a life that is going to be approved needs continuity, some character, order, and less change. No wonder, then, that Aristotle and Plato, among others who thought very hard about how to live a life, concluded that we needed some shape and symmetry, some form and organization, to our wants, motives, intentions, and drives, just to make living agreeable to ourselves.

For centuries the term "virtues" has been applied to the organized ways that all of us can modulate and control our changeable and restless lives. At the least we can say that virtues are not quite natural, not quite native. They are acquired, even learned. But what, actually, are they? Perhaps a contrast will be useful. If I come to someone's rescue when he or she is being accosted by a thug, an observer might say: "How brave! You could have run away." Indeed, it may have been easy to do just that, and I did not. There are two possibilities here. One is that my action was totally impulsive, almost an accident, and surely not a clue to the way I usually am. My disposition may actually be to avoid trouble, look the other way, and generally stay away from anything that is dangerous, uncertain, and difficult. I could say that I know myself to be cowardly. Maybe I cringe over the prospects, debate endlessly with myself, and seldom take any action I consider rash. Therefore, my action in aiding another person was not in character, for I was not brave and surely not courageous. Moreover, I am unlikely to do anything like that again.

The other possibility is more appealing. Suppose that my action was typical of me, so that others might say, "That's just like him—always taking risks for others." Then others begin to think differently about me. Then they have the right to say, "He is truly courageous." For being courageous and brave is not a matter of doing something once. When we speak of a person as being courageous, we mean that he or she is characteristically that way. A certain kind of invariableness is known about him or her; he or she is prone to be like that in every circumstance where there is peril or need. Doing something just once does not count for very much if one is asking whether a person is punctual, patient, just, or courageous. In all such instances, we have to be sure that the disposition of the person is established, and that a pattern of behavior is likely, before we call the person just, courageous, or patient.

What we mean by a virtue, then, is an acquired disposition or inclination that will make behavior predictable and regular. In earlier times, virtues were also described as habits—not meaning mechanical or thoughtless, routine or compulsive behavior but, rather, behavior that could be counted on. People who had the reputation of being wise about human existence got that reputation because they saw clearly what most of us have seen only dimly. They saw that everyone needed to have courage as a standing capacity and way of coping with the uncertain world, the future, and the flux around them. No one can foresee very much, so we all must be ready for whatever happens. Courage is a kind of readiness or self-preparation to manage ourselves when the world and society begin to shift around us.

It is almost as if courage is that kind of virtue, that kind of self-formation, that matches up with the lottery-like character of the world. Even Christians, who believe in God's providence and abiding love, do not escape this random way of the world. Rain falls on the just and the unjust; accidents, war, death, and separations make for extensive dislocations and radically novel situations to which we must adjust. Obviously, without courage, one could scarcely live at all. If one is cowardly, cringing, and timorous, the world itself begins to look totally bleak and dismal. Small wonder, then, that the ancients thought courage was "cardinal," meaning that this virtue was primary and fundamental, one upon which all kinds of other factors depended. As important as we might think politeness might be in some circumstances, it is so only in some circumstances, whereas courage is important in all circumstances. Hence the latter has been thought to be, and is, a cardinal virtue, a kind of hinge, upon which all kinds of other concerns depend.

Of course, there are other fundamental habits that are needed. Precisely because we are so changeable—so likely both to hate and to love, to vacillate in enthusiasm depending upon humidity, heat, and health—all of us need a kind of personal monitor, a kind of control. We do get that in part by the fact that laws and customs, police and parents, restrain us from the outside. But this works only very crudely and only under some circumstances. Waxing hot and cold, wavering between lust and indifference, wobbling between drunkenness and abstinence, we soon become very unruly and wretched people. How much better it might be to have the commands rising up from within!

It is not surprising that a physical life that will allow us to eat endlessly, to enjoy voluptuous pleasure, and to be avaricious for goods and money also allows us to become penurious and stingy, unable to love anybody at all, and finally even mean and thoughtless toward others. When one becomes aware of the extremes that are possible, then it also becomes clear, as it did to early moralists, that being temperate is a sheer necessity. Temperance is also an acquired disposition, an acquired preference for moderation and for the mean between the extremes. Rather than letting appetite, satiation, or boredom randomly dictate one's behavior, it seems right and sensible to moderate one's satisfaction from within. Temperance is a name for a regularized way of governing personal impulses and habits.

Something like this could also be said about learning to be just. Oftentimes we can improvise our behavior in a chancy way and come out right. But an action that takes place just by chance or only once is not a great credit to anyone. If I treat someone with respect when everyone else is doing the same, then my action will be a matter of accidental conformity to a social pattern. But if I treat another person with propriety in circumstances that are not to my advantage, then a kind of character is asked of me. Having character is a matter of being disposed, being likely, and being predictable when circumstances are not always conducive. For the very reason that the world is as it is, full of uncertainties and unpredictable, and because it often rewards the unjust and the rapacious, justice as a personality qualification is sorely needed. Courage, temperance, and justice are not just accidental points of view, useful for one time and not for another. They are not relative or pertinent to just one society, one epoch, or one culture. Instead, they are needed because of the way people always are and the way physical and social contexts are.

The possibilities for injustice are endless, and they keep cropping up no matter whether the government is democratic, fascistic, or anarchical. Most of us suffer injustices and also commit them. None of us is so fortunate as to be without the need to become temperate, courageous, and just. If we do not become these things, then our lives disintegrate and make no sense at all. Who among us could ever decide to be a coward? Certainly, being without virtues is not a state that we can be taught or that we entertain with a clear mind and full awareness of the consequences. Instead we lapse into vices, just as an architect lapses into a poor design. No one builds a poor structure by trying to do so. No one who knows what it means to think thinks badly on purpose. A building that does not succeed and thoughts that do not hang together bring their own penalties. So do badly conceived lives. Virtues are the very means of bringing lives into a kind of rightness, a kind of moral sense, and this is why they are so momentous to all of us. Once we have thought about the virtues, they become very hard to ignore. They look like the minimal essentials for a life that is expected to have desirable results.

III

A contrasting state for all of us is easily understood. One does not have to be an apostle oneself to see with Paul how absurd lives become when they are full of pride, envy, murder, strife, malice, deceit, gossip, and ruthlessness (see Romans 1). Long ago, thoughtful people—indeed, wise ones— also saw that there were some terrible vices into which we could fall and thereby wreck our lives. If you so lived that envy became highly characteristic, then all sorts of things would go wrong. Envy, after a while, also becomes a habit, a kind of regular feature. And a terrible thing about it is that it begins to destroy an aptness for gracious activity and just assessment of others. It destroys peace of mind by always making us think that others are happier or more fortunate. It puts us in the insidious state of wanting to erase all the differences. It whets our appetite for what others have and are, and it turns life into a pursuit of more vanities. An envious person begins to look differently after a bit, for envy is very difficult to disguise. Worst of all, envy does not stand up to our own gaze. If we start to examine ourselves when envious, we can hardly bear to look. This is why envy, when it truly becomes a vice and an established way of comporting oneself, diminishes a person considerably. One of envy's first features is that it hardly allows any thinking about oneself. Thoughtfulness becomes the enemy, and with the lessening of thought comes the lessening of the person.

Other vices are like this, too. For example, if we allow ourselves to become lustful or gluttonous, it is very hard to be satisfied with ordinary pleasures and ordinary food. Lust for the extremes breeds a dissatisfaction with the middle range of pleasures that is otherwise the norm. If two people love each other over a long period and are temperate, they can find satisfaction with small accomplishments, with continuing loyalties, and with faithful attention to, and tolerance for, personal eccentricities. But once a lover demands the extraordinary in every embrace, then nothing less than tingling sensations and maximal enthusiasm will suffice. So, too, with the appetites for food and drink. The person who loses the capacity to be pleased by ordinary food soon has to make extravagant demands. Everything has to be excessive and ever novel.

The world itself, its persons, its foods, its circumstances, is not so bountiful that it can keep up with such meretricious and restless desire. We become meretricious ourselves when, instead of finding satisfaction and rest, we create ever more and more exquisite desires. Then we become driven people, urged on in ceaseless pursuits, with no peace for our souls. One of the debilitating features of modern life is that this endless push for satisfaction is now available to large numbers of people. Thus it looks as if it is natural and the standard point of departure for the good life. When everybody begins to do it, this mode of life looks irresistible. Even Christians of our day have not dared to criticize or to evaluate this freedom that masquerades as the license to be creative and to develop one's personality. But such compliance is befuddling, and it has caused many people to lose sight of the plain fact that there are other moral criteria and that these criteria are not a consequence of dogmatism or arbitrary moral authority. Vices are as clear negative instances as virtues are positive instances. Both are standards by which to judge our behavior.

It is hard to imagine anyone choosing to be sick. If we find someone like that, we are certain that there is an equally strange explanation, for sickness is never, under ordinary conditions, voluntary. We cannot understand anyone who chooses to be wretched, for happiness is what we seek, not its opposite. In moral matters it is safe to say that we fall into downright folly when we believe that all standards are individual and that everyone's life has to be an essay into the morally unknown. On the contrary, who with clear thought and awareness of himself or herself could ever choose to be cowardly? Who could choose lust? gluttony? envy? folly? and sloth of the spirit? All these are vices, just as honesty, temperance, prudence, courage, and more are virtues. We do not have to invent such notions for ourselves, nor are we the victims of others' imposition of values. When we endorse virtues and eschew vices, we are merely acknowledging how things are with all of us. Once more, these make up that grammar of life which no one person has invented and no one culture has prescribed. They set the boundaries of sense for lives anywhere and at any time.

If a person refused to obey the rules that make up the grammar of a language, we would not quite know what to say. The fact is that to speak the language at all requires that one get tenses, word order, and a host of other things straight. One has no choice. We can say with confidence to those who balk at the grammar of a language, "You can learn it," "You must learn it," and "You will learn it." "Can," "must," and "will"! In learning a language, everyone can master the grammar because it comes with the words and their use. If people want words but not grammar, we can say that they must learn the grammar, for the words mean little or nothing until we get sentences, paragraphs, arguments, and discourse. The "must" thus takes care of itself. Surely, then, they will learn the grammar in spite of themselves. Before one recognizes it, the grammar is in the very command one has of the vocabulary and all the uses of words.

Moral life, when thought about in terms of the elementary virtues and vices, is a little like this. Contrary to what most people say, morality can be learned. There is an air of skepticism that pervades our society on such matters. We easily conclude that morals are relative; if we say that often enough and long enough, it looks as if morals and values are merely asserted in this circumstance or by this person or that group. We begin to think that morals are made up as we go along, that morals have no more authority than we choose to give them. Then we do become skeptical, and we are inclined to drift along without any decisiveness. We let circumstances push us, and we wallow in uncertainty instead of invoking the certainties we actually have already. This is the very way that a life becomes meaningless and random. Our life becomes like a word does if it has no grammar—it dangles there without connections and without meaning much of anything.

But virtues and vices are already there as a big part of the grammar of life; they are already laid down. That grammar is not an imposition upon one's freedom any more than the grammar of French or English is an unwanted burden. To know the grammar of life is like knowing the grammar of a living language; it enables and empowers one to make sense. In fact, it does not tell us what to do any more than English grammar tells us what to say, but it does tell us *how* to live just as the constructions of a language inform us *how* to express ourselves.

We can learn this grammar of life if we pay a little attention. Obviously, "can" implies that every one of us is able and has the capacity. Think about how we learn the grammar of our native language. Very few people can state the grammatical rules that govern their speaking and writing. Nonetheless, they do obey those rules; otherwise, no one could understand them at all. The ability to become grammatical in one's speech does not depend completely upon understanding grammar abstractly or being qualified to discuss the reasons for the rules in a cogent way. One does not need to be a grammarian in order to be grammatical. This is why we say that something as important as making sense of one's life is not completely dependent upon having a theory of morals or upon having all the theological nuances under command. The sense of our lives is sometimes contingent upon how we fashion ourselves emotionally and how we manage ourselves morally. If we can become temperate, courageous, and just, we go a long way toward making a life

that bears up under the human traffic. If we avoid intemper-
ance, malice, wrath, and gnawing envy among the many
vices, we discover the grammar of life in actual situations
where it is embedded and readily accessible.

But every person will and must discover the grammar of
the language he or she speaks. Grammar is so much a part
of our language that to absorb even the simplest ways of talking is already to imbibe the grammar. We take it in unwit-
tingly and almost without effort. And a few experiences of
not making ourselves understood soon conspire to force us
to speak according to the rules. The business of living is not
quite like that. We can neglect and refuse the grammar of life
for a very long time indeed. We sometimes will our down-
fall and make our own perdition. Most of us also learn pride
and try to make a virtue of our independence and individuality. We refuse help and deny our need. This is why human living after a while becomes so solemn (but also so sar-
donically absurd and ridiculous). It is as if we have to live
with what we have made of ourselves, and the prospect is
seldom pleasing. We can for a time make our own rules, and
we do. This is why the learning of the grammar of life, the
way of the virtues, often comes slowly and after many trials
and failures. Often it is pressed on us by the vicissitudes of
a lifetime. Sometimes, unfortunately, we come to ourselves
when it is too late.

We do get used to despair. Some of us become cynics and
pessimists and think that all of existence is a big joke. Or we
derive the silly consolation, which is the only kind available
after a while, that says this is the way life is—bitter, short,
and pointless. So the grammar of life indeed "can" be sur-
mised. Whether it will be or not depends upon one's clarity
of mind about oneself.

IV

There is one range of considerations we have omitted thus far that deserves longer consideration than we will be able to give it here. While I am not retracting anything said about how sense (and we could also say significance, worth, and meaning) gets integrated into one's life stream, something else has to be noted about making sense of one's life before God. It should be patent by now that one simple picture that we get from a superficially conceived account is being side-stepped. That shallow notion is that we first encounter some teachings, then ascertain whether they make sense—for example, whether they are true, false, meaningful, or relevant at all—then respond to them with our emotions, will, and behavior. This way of describing human living puts the theory first; the abstract statement of facts, rules, or duties is in the dominant position. Then the "sense" is supposed to be chiefly in the teachings, while the rest—deeds, emotions, and willing—is part of the application or the practice. Then we get familiar distinctions like theory and practice, teachings and use, abstract and concrete. Instead of all that, these pages have declared that our lives themselves lose sense and quality when we do not achieve the standing dispositions that are virtues, in contrast to the vagrant tendencies that we call vices. The point is that people, not just words or teachings, also have to make sense. Modification and managing of ourselves is a good part of the wisdom of the moralists as well as the wisdom of the Lord. When we put all the stress on teachings as the sense bearers, we tend to neglect the very qualities of our personal life that will truly ruin us if we do not give them heed.

Now we return again to a consideration of the differences that Christian teachings make. Making sense morally is something like a minimum natural requirement. However, there is a kind of difficulty that is peculiar to moral striving itself, and Christian literature writes that difficulty very large. Most of us are tempted by the thought of moral improvement to think that we can secure our own judgment of our rightness. We are prone to think that we can establish ourselves in righteousness and that we can overcome the wasting and gnawing sense of not being good enough by moral effort. All of us do want an established and certain guarantee of our worth, our validity, as persons. The more sensitive and concerned we are about ourselves, the more we yearn for that. Thus making sense of ourselves by the virtues—and the emotions—is not an optional and accidental matter at all.

But Christian teaching tells us plainly that doing the works of the law will not establish our righteousness, and furthermore that God, who is the ultimate judge, will not be persuaded by our achievements either. This kind of teaching does not dangle loosely over human life. For it does appear to be the case that anyone who works hard on being virtuous finds the goal continually receding. What the Bible says in general about all of us can be discovered in particular about oneself. We are in a rather poor position to make our own righteousness. We can always criticize ourselves and see that often we have done good, not because we like goodness, but because we want the praise we get for it. Double-mindedness and duplicity can pervade our morals, too.

More than this, we can begin to despair about the possibility of moral success. Nothing fits a person so well, so exquisitely, as does guilt. Here, then, is another kind of emotion, one that is hurtful and pervasive. It can bring about the mood of despair and an ever-deeper sloth of the spirit, when no effort, not even an upright and upbuilding one, seems quite worth the cost. Guilt of a responsible sort occurs typically in those who care a great deal about themselves. Such guilt is not just a psychological peculiarity. It, too, belongs to the working out of a life.

Now, however, the Bible's teachings also can get a grip on

each of us. For this guilt is part of what is implied by the notion that works-righteousness is not enough. The Scriptures flatter us with the thought that the eternal is already planted in our hearts, and our restlessness with both our unrighteousness and our righteousness is a token of the need for something more. And that something more is God himself. For the God of the Law and the God of Jesus Christ are the same God. The New Testament is the story of how Jesus Christ is a kind of passive righteousness, a righteousness that is given and not achieved. That righteous God forgives us for our lacks and failures, our immorality as well as our morality. Righteousness is imputed to us; and, before God and ourselves, we no longer have to grovel in need or fester in guilt.

Right here, then, thinking about making sense of our lives takes on a different hue. The notion that righteousness can be imputed, that one can be passive and receive the fundamental kind of rightness, is certainly a formidable and difficult one to comprehend. But this much does ensue. The motive for becoming virtuous and good no longer has to be to please God or even to please oneself. Anyway, neither of these quite works. Instead, one can do all of this simply by making sense as one goes along. One's own life is more tolerable if one is temperate and courageous; one does not then sow more seeds of regret, fear, self-contempt, and dismay. Somehow, morality can start by being just that and nothing more.

Furthermore, Christians, too, have to be courageous just to get along in the everyday world. Likewise, no one is exempted from the need for temperance. And the presence of other people simply requires us, Christian or not, to be just and to give everyone his or her due. The issue is still that a life does not make sense unless the person begins to qualify himself or herself. We cannot let ourselves be completely uncultivated. Furthermore, we need the action made by our decisions and deeds—what Luther called "active righteousness"—just to stay alive. The need is natural and unremitting. But once one is a Christian, the works become a consequence of the new confidence, the new certainty, and the new righteousness that faith provides. Whereas previously our striving for virtues and our battle against vices augmented our own sense of worthlessness and despair, now it is as if we are free of having to use morals for nonmoral ends. We need no longer be in despair even if we fail, for the Christian gospel is the story of God's love, which justifies us when we truly believe and trust in God, not just when we succeed morally.

Therefore, there can be no diminution of concern for making sense of one's life. But it is now the case that morality is not expected to save any one of us. We do not ask so much of ourselves or of our moral efforts. Besides, there is another kind of germane consideration. Our world is full of people who are confused and frustrated by the existence of a certain kind of moral disagreement. Many of us are inclined to think that morals make no sense at all unless it is possible to reach an agreement on them. This happens because we tend to think that we are moral only when we are deciding issues of right and wrong, goodness and badness. Then we suppose that anyone's view is as good as anyone else's, which sounds as if morals do not amount to anything. But after thinking about it in the manner noted in this chapter, we begin to understand that every one of us needs to be qualified in order to make his or her own way. Instead of being frustrated by the disagreements, we now see that amid all the shortcomings of our moral views and the uncertainty of thinking about the world and its happenings in moral terms, we ourselves can still become moral. The world, too, needs people who will be temperate, kind, patient, and courageous amid its confusions and uncertainties.

Many times, whether Christians or unbelievers, we will be unable to see what we should do. We will be in doubt about whether we took the right decision or did the right thing for another person. It is not as if such questions have an answer in the mind of God and the task of faith is to find it out. No, the point is rather that living in such a world as God has made requires us to be decisive and to make up our minds, often right on the spot. This is why we have to be temperate, thoughtful, considerate, just, and ever courageous. As people we have to be prepared. And those virtues are like ways open to us that will enable us to make sense as we go along.

Christians have dared to think, too, that love is a new disposition that believing in God allows us to enjoy. Of course, charity as it is described in the New Testament does not quite seem to be what we would call a natural love or an attraction. It is more comprehensive; it accounts for enemies, aliens, strangers, and many others who are very difficult to love. Such a disposition looks like something that comes only when you can truly relax your striving and can have your solace in the thought that God already loves you, unlovely though you may be. When you have faith in such a God, it is as if the faith rooted in you allows that disposition to grow and to generate a new life. Furthermore, love gives you another source of motives to be kind, temperate, and without envy or avarice. Love itself is satisfying; it is often its own reward. All the other virtues become easier, almost as if they were fruits of God's Spirit in us.

These, then, are some of the considerations that bear upon our common human tasks. If we only had to make sense on paper, we could probably write out a fairly coherent proposal. But the human agenda is more important than that. Our lives can fail, and do; but they also can succeed, and do. If we have spoken at all correctly, we have described ways to make sense both with our emotions and with our virtues. We can now turn to a parallel kind of consideration about the human will.

CHAPTER FOUR

MAKING SENSE WITH THE WILL

I

All of us know about all kinds of wishes. When we were children, we had wishes that were short and vivid, yet totally captivating. Sometimes adults stay childlike and have a wish today and then forget it tomorrow. There are wishes that die in being stated, there are wishes of which we are ashamed, there are wishes that we outgrow, and there are wishes that outlast our days and our lives. Knowing what we ought to wish is a good part of the wisdom of life. If we never know what to wish that is worthy and long-standing, that endures and outlasts a momentary enthusiasm, then we have a disaster in the making.

We are tempted to offer excuses for this great range of differences in wishing and in willing; then our thinking about ourselves begins to lose discipline and order, too. We were close to saying earlier that there are many ethical and political decisions, many personal choices, about which we are deeply uncertain. We do not deny the large range of uncertainty in all kinds of empirical and practical matters, social and personal. However, that does not mean that all deliberation is pointless or that all concerns about oneself and one's qualities are vain. Not everything is relative, and not everything is a matter of whimsy. Virtues are within our power, and so, too, are vices. Virtues become dispositions after a while. If we ask how one acquires a virtue like being temperate, the answer is by choosing a middle way, rather than yielding to extremes. This is an activity. We do it. If someone does not know that dispositions are attained by actually doing courageous things repeatedly, by practicing temperance regularly, and by making punctuality a standard feature of one's day, and so on, then one is, in the words of Aristotle, "a complete ignoramus" (*Nicomachean Ethics*, Book III). Activities add up after a while. If we are careless and thoughtless about ourselves, we can slip into bad habits that will dispose us in ways that bring harm and disintegration.

If what we have said rings true, then we have no excuse in the thought that our character is such that we cannot care, be just, or be loving. For people are, in many cases, responsible for their disorderly and hapless lives. If they are profligate, careless, and thoughtless, or never make a decision, they may very well be responsible for their lack of character, since activities themselves give a person character. As we have noted, the business of becoming a worthy person— even self-approved—is fraught with difficulties. The kind of moral concern we are talking about admits to one desperate fact, namely, that if a person acts unjustly long enough, then that person's character does become formed and he or she can no longer become just by merely wanting to be just. If one has lived a careless and profligate life, it may be impossible to avoid illness. But the moral concern we have been urging also goes back further than this by suggesting that as we start our serious reflection about ourselves, we can avoid profligacy, injustice, and cowardliness. Instead, we can practice love, justice, and other virtues and acquire another kind of character, one that will weave sense and decency into the very texture of our daily life.

Of course, this is also the heart of Christian training, but with a difference or two. For the emphasis there is also on the forming of the individual; if we succeed at that, then other matters take care of themselves. Some of us may act out of ignorance and think that we are, therefore, not liable for what we do, but in all likelihood we are responsible for our own ignorance. Once we begin to see this feature of ourselves, we learn a use for the expression that says we can act "in virtue of" this or that character trait. Being ignorant is within our competence, but so is being knowledgeable. Being preoccupied with what the New Testament calls "flesh," or with money, getting ahead of others, or easy gratifications, will also indispose us after a while and make us unable to seek the things of God. Then we cannot do the things we want, nor can we love graciously, give ourselves with bounty, or live with enthusiasm and hope. Christian teaching also pushes us to the thought that we are responsible for what we make of ourselves. But it is the theme of the New Testament that God, out of unbounded mercy and love, simply declares that a new spirit and a new disposition can dwell in us. If we dare to live that faith, then we will be converted and radically changed; then each of us can be made alive by an unheard-of righteousness. But we are responsible for letting ourselves be converted. If we do not yield here, we will live in hostility to the very things we want most.

A major connection between ourselves and moral worth, also between ourselves and Christian righteousness, is the will. Not even that passive righteousness given to us in Jesus Christ can be ours unless we seek it. More than this, though, is the fact that no one of us can even be a person, be a real self, without a will. Without being a person and being able, therefore, to know ourselves even a little, there is nothing to our daily existence. Just how the will gives sense to our multifarious tasks is the burden of this chapter.

II

Willing something is not quite an overt activity. Typically, one cannot watch anyone doing a bit of willing. It is not done by any visible organ, and it is not something that, in itself, occupies one's attention or dominates one's enthusiasm. For example, if I will to understand something, say a mathematical problem, I spend my effort and concern not on the willing but on the mathematics. My concern is with the tangle in thought, not with the willing. It is likely that no one sees any willing in and of itself, but a spectator could easily remark upon my single-mindedness if I let a mathematical problem exclude everything else.

Willing is not, therefore, a hidden activity always going on in each person. It is not the case that each of us is always willing in the same manner as we are breathing. Indeed, I keep breathing day after day, but I am not interested in knowing much about it; I do not ordinarily have to be aware of breathing in order to do it properly. Willing is not like breathing. Willing is not quite a skill; and one does not do it slowly, rapidly, automatically, or even carelessly. Yet we have a great number of uses for that word "willing." To become clearer about them, we can begin with a kind of fault that most of us can quickly discover in ourselves. Then we can perhaps discern how willing fits in with the broader aspects of our daily life.

Who of us does not know how absurd we become when we choose incompatible goals? If someone says that he or she wants above all else to help others but then also begins to live in ways that only allow a concern with becoming wealthy, a contradiction is set up that makes for real folly. The point is that often we do not have to say contradictory things to begin to behave in ways that are contradictory and self-defeating. Willing in a way that brings help to others requires that we push our own interests aside in preference for those of others. However, becoming rich will often presuppose that one keeps one's own interests paramount, even at the expense of others. If I say I want to be learned and know what is what, I must let ignorance be my target to attack; everything else takes second place. However, while saying all that, I can only make a fool of myself if I now begin to seek eminence with great zest. It is not that learning and eminence are always at odds, any more than wealth and helpfulness are, but it is very hard to will both sides of those pairs together.

This is because willing, while not quite an activity in itself, is a matter of decisiveness, of choice, and of determination and, actually, the making of oneself. We cannot do everything or be everything. More than this, living becomes serious after a while, not because the choices are so momentous but because our own lives are. What we will, want, and wish are not only clues to what we are as persons and selves, they are the very means of becoming selves. Thus the person who has no self-understanding and no self-knowledge might well suffer these needs because there is nothing yet in place to know or to understand.

Most of us would like to share the flattery of the world that says people are very complicated and hence difficult to know. We all rather like to hear that, for it makes the obscurity we have about our motives, purposes, and intentions sound justified. Certainly, many of us are unclear about what we want to do, what we are capable of, and even what we like and dislike. This is not simply because we have so many likes, or because the world is changing so rapidly, or that the variables in human behavior are so many.

Even in the sciences dealing with humans and their behavior, it is often said that obscurities and a lack of confirmed general laws are due to the infinite complexities of the human brain and to the confounding possibilities of human behavior. All of us have read those public laments that say we now need only to multiply our research facilities and find more money to get at the mysteries of human life and behavior so the sciences will be truly helpful and conclusive. But this is more flattery about ourselves, and likely to make us forget the one thing we need. Indeed it is true that there is very little self-knowledge; it is also the case that useful knowledge of personality is at a minimum. However, this way of describing our need dooms all of us to perpetual postponement of satisfaction. For it suggests that eventually all those complexities will be matched by a stunning kind of knowledge about personality, a superpsychology that will give us certainty, clarity, and insight about motives and prospects. But, barring its attainment (which is decades away, so we are told) we all have to be content with human bumbling, with one conjecture after another, and with the dismal admission that human life is a continual accommodation to variability and change.

This is like asserting that human life makes little or no sense as we live it, yet it cannot be made clearer and more satisfying until we have a science of humanity. And there is little prospect of that even in the remote future. Furthermore, lives will not make sense, because we have no self-knowledge; and, ostensibly, we cannot have self-knowledge until we have scientific knowledge of the human personality. Surely there is more than a tissue of absurdity in all this momentous talk. Worse, though, is the fact that ethically and religiously concerned people also become intimidated and begin to believe that morals and faith are poorly grounded, maybe in an antiquated view of man. Restlessness and fever begin to take over. The sense-providing features of moral and religious living are neglected altogether, and enthusiasm for objective knowledge is continually stimulated.

But this is misguided. Furthermore, it makes the task of becoming a self depend on knowledge that no one has. Therefore, another assessment of moral and religious concerns is in order. To return to the matter of the will, we can say that by willing, wanting, and wishing—especially if we do so steadily and for a long time—the self comes into existence. For if we choose with decisiveness, if we become determined to have something or to be something, then that very decisiveness makes us into a self that can be known. The chief reason for the lack of self-understanding is not human complexity and the infinitude of possibilities; instead, it is the plain fact that there is little or nothing to know. If I have willed to be just over a long period of time, so that justice is now a disposition, then I am not up against a vague array of impulses, never being sure which will dominate. If I have become courageous by habit, there will be something clear about myself. I will be able to avoid random and tentative activities and be more confident of what I should do.

In all of this, though, it is a kind of moral and religious decisiveness that constitutes the self. The willing of goodness, of goals, of godliness, of making something of oneself—these are the very means of being able to understand and know oneself. We do not need to languish because there is no general theory of what a person is; we do not have to lament the poverty of the sciences about human nature. Each of us has a kind of power and authority in our capacity to will, even to want and to wish, that is close at hand.

We will now consider another facet or two of willing that should make all this clearer.

III

If a person is always restless and anxious, there can be no resoluteness of will. With little or no will, there is nothing clear or definitive about such a person. Sometimes it is hard to know whether the lack of volition comes first and the restless anxiety follows, or the reverse. However, we need not decide such questions in order to say that surely the two go together. A sign of being weak-willed is to shift from one thing to another. Having a will for this, then for that, in end-less succession, is really to have no conclusiveness and no character at all. Such a mode of life spells chaos after a while. Soon one does not know what will satisfy, and a lifetime can be spent in meaningless pursuits. Contrariwise, if one is pleased by too many things in turn, then one is soon pleased by hardly anything at all.

Something like this happens to us when we spend ourselves in preoccupation with pleasure. It is one of the strangest facts about us that most of us recognize that being pleasure-oriented is a kind of human travesty, and also that pleasure is good. None of us can live without an interest in being pleased or without pleasures, for pleasures, as well as pains, discomforts, and frustrations, give us clues on how to behave. We give pleasure to others in the confidence that we are doing well by them. We find pleasure in music, in food, in marriage. And the pleasure itself is a harbinger of the worth of what we do. We are not in a position to give up pleasure altogether. At the same time, we find it sad if a child of ours chooses pleasure and nothing else. To become a connoisseur of foods, persons, and books only for the pleasure they bring is to fail to understand ourselves, on the one hand, and foods, persons, and books, on the other.

The odd thing about pleasure is that to seek it always is to spoil the person. In a somewhat vague way, most of us know that about ourselves and about others. Gratifications and delights have a way of fashioning our will. Make delectation your goal, and it is as if you have to keep yourself restless and always poised for a new range of possibilities. One cannot settle into anything or be circumscribed in desire and wish, for then satisfaction may not come. A kind of worldly wisdom begins to take over, and it requires that one live in abeyance and a little lightly. The effect upon the person then becomes pronounced. For one cannot then live for one thing; instead, one has to will everything and stay wide open to the future.

Think how hard it is then to keep a promise, let alone live in such a way that one's life fulfills a promise. If one takes a marriage vow to love until death, the supposition is that the promise is something one wills. It proposes that one can so live that an entire lifetime of energy, change, children, illness, even sufferings, can be governed and disciplined so that one will not need to reestablish oneself or change radically in order to cope with life. Once we let pleasures govern our considerations, however, the hold of the promise is weakened and our resolutions have to be altered. Soon the self scarcely knows itself, and the promise is not something to be kept. Unfortunately, a promise that is conditional, that will be kept only for a while, until the advantage of greater pleasure is offered, is not a promise at all. And if one thinks at all about such matters, it is true that once one gives up on the promise, one cannot be certain of how one will feel ten years later. For the self is then in flux, and one cannot predict what one will become. Some people want to posit restlessness and arbitrariness of will as the new wisdom. But the moral and religious tradition will have it that we are made in God's image and that constancy, fidelity, and promising will keep that image burnished and clear.

So, choosing pleasure will cost us the lovely opportunity of willing one thing. It will deprive us of the confidence, character, and surety within which we can become true selves, something of which we can be proud. None of us knows the coming historical conditions, the future state of our health, or the sufferings we will have to bear; hence, we cannot even begin to predict what will give us pleasure in the long tomorrows. One can suppose that the countless serious reflections about the limitation of seeking pleasures must have a great deal to do with the discovery of this very logic of human life. None of us wants to be a victim of occurrences. We cannot will to be the flotsam that just moves with the waters, cast hither and yon. To have a will at all means that we have to deliberate and manage our own lives. Willing entails promising and deciding. When we become conscious of what we are not and of what we can be, then the self is formed. We become recognizable, to ourselves as well as to others, when we consciously and purposively give form to those vagrant impulses, wants, drives, and temptations that otherwise elicit our behavior.

Something like this is at stake in the notion that the will can become a "good" will. For willing is something we can do. It is a capacity we all have, and it demands an exercise and a use. If we let that capacity slide away from us, we destroy ourselves. A kind of moral suicide will overtake us if we do not concern ourselves about ourselves. Besides, living adds up to nothing and loses its bearings when there is no self as its center. To will restlessly and chaotically is not, finally, to will at all. It is to lose that capacity rather than to strengthen it. Having a good will is to will steadily and long, to will in such a way that the weight of a lifetime will not break up the self. Indeed, a good will allows the self to come into existence, to gain strength, to know itself, and to be content with what is there. All kinds of factors then begin to come together. Instead of relentlessly spying out the possibilities of pleasures in new companions, situations, and experiences, instead of living with attendant stress and anxiety, the person molded by a good will can now be made secure by a promise. Such a person of formed will now discovers pleasure where he or she least expected it—in monotony, in suffering, in doing what one must, even in being temperate, courageous, patient, and long-suffering.

When such a "good" will is exercised, the self is being saved, rather than dissipated and spent. There is even a sly kind of advantage that is like an unmerited gift. For the sense we begin to make when the will is collected and focused brings another kind of satisfaction altogether, a quiet contentment in being who one is and in becoming what one is making of oneself. This happiness is not a matter of collecting pleasures and being certain that there are more and more pleasures as over against their opposites; it is, instead, a kind of concord between the will and all the rest of what makes up one's life. Rather than being dissatisfied with who one is, a good will allows one to will with enthusiasm what one is. No longer does one droop with regret and remorse. One can relish one's days and live vigorously.

Isn't this the point, then, that instead of willing an abstract good or a general aim we learn to take our daily life seriously? The locus of the good is in the self. We will to be the self that in one respect we already are. And that singleness of aim is intrinsically rewarding.

IV

In the heart of all of us there is a space occupied by the working of the mysteries of our lives, and that little space is tinged with sadness. For few of us have assurance on the things that matter most. We all seem to be close to something deep here, something that tries us, and something in which, if we fail, we will create horrors for ourselves. As concerns what is mysterious and strange about ourselves, we are not as naive as we sometimes seem. Certainly we know that we cannot read out of any book the wisdom needed for our own lives. The surface of life is full of exceedingly trivial little waves of thought that create excitement and a kind of movement of small interest, but all of that creates only a buzz, a vibration or two, a diverting stir in our consciousness. Then those deeper mysteries of our everyday life assert themselves again. The increase of thought here increases our sorrow.

There is a kind of surface glamour of existence that holds us in thrall. Yet we all know how shallow the moods of optimism are when they are stirred by easy conformity to social standards or are produced by good looks that have not yet faded or good health that seems boundless. No life can quite vouch for itself. No mood can be made permanent, and no facts in the world will stay as they are. Even knowledge of the world will pass away. No wonder, then, that when life becomes difficult to handle, we show forth our thralldom by wanting to change our circumstances. But it seldom helps very much. The most important change is the one we are exceedingly reluctant to make, that is to say, a change in our life, in its direction and attitudes. We do have to assume a role in respect to ourselves. After all, we are not just material objects, directed from the outside. We are spiritual beings, and the more spiritual we are, the more dependent we are upon our will. So we have to will the good and the one thing needful.

For centuries a kind of wisdom on this matter has surfaced again and again. We have to will what is and not indulge in silly expectations and vain hopes. Governing the will is a very taxing business, but it is absolutely essential. We must know what the world is, what the prospects are, and live accordingly. Anything else becomes folly. So, realism about oneself and a willingness to do what is appropriate and right are minimal requirements. Since what is being said here is obvious, the reader might easily conclude that all this talk is trivial. But it is not.

The wisdom of morality is plainly on the side of the good and strong will that each of us must establish. None of us has the right to give up before trying. The essence of the thought here is, simply, that we cannot be true persons if we are frivolous, restless, thoughtless, or will-less about ourselves. Hence, we must not despair of ourselves; we cannot give up. We have to will ourselves, not hate ourselves; we must choose to be ourselves with some relish and piquancy, or we will dribble away our lifetime.

Right here is where the disciplining of the will begins. We have to give up disparate goals and learn to concentrate upon what is of true moment, and we have to do so with passion. Now we return to an issue discussed earlier, in Chapter 2. There we alluded to a difference between an emotion (like anger), which takes an object or has a target, and a mood (like irritability), which is precipitated by almost anything. Someone who is readily excited to impatience or vexation, who loses control when a situation does not deserve it, is moody. The point is that a mood, be it cheerfulness, sadness, or irritability, makes the whole world its target. Anything and everything can evoke a response. But now consider a passion. An emotion has a specific target, but a passion, like a mood, is really carried by the individual, and it is, therefore, appropriate to everything. Marital love can become a passion, so it can survive aging, illness, the loss of youth, and even the attenuation of sexuality. But if one asks what secures a passion like that, it certainly is the fact that people can will a promise and stay faithful until death parts them!

A passion is voluntary. One determines to love everlastingly; that kind of love is not an emotion, triggered only by circumstances. An emotion is seldom voluntary. Emotions like fear, anger, and disappointment are short-term and are usually produced by external circumstances. But passions are typically long-term, and they are held in place by resolution and avowals. Furthermore, like moods, they are inclusive and tend to envelop large areas of interest and concern. Unlike moods, they are not symptoms of the ill health of an individual. A mood overwhelms, whereas a passion enables a person to conquer circumstances.

To win over the world one needs a passion that will keep one in its grip. Knowledge never quite does that. But what kind of passion is even conceivably so powerful and formidable? We have already noted that moral passion is very close to being like that. For the ethical passion that infuses one's life and its qualities is a pure one. We never live long enough to exhaust it, and we can have it whether we are rich or poor, dull or intelligent, sick or healthy. It is a passion that can carry us through all circumstances, and it will enable us to bear just about anything. Furthermore, we may try to will intelligence, wealth, and health, but none of these turn out to be worth very much unless the person who wills them is worthy. This reminds one of a remark by the German philosopher Kant, who said that ethics is not the science that makes one happy but the science that makes one worthy of happiness. So, too, with being zealous for being alive, for being a self, for being a personality. Without a passion (even a love) for oneself, any other gift or achievement soon loses its worth. The opposite of this passion, this willed enthusiasm for becoming a worthy person, is surely that frightful mood "despair." Once we are in the grip of despair, life becomes vanity. Nothing so quickly rubs out enthusiastic diligence for living as does despair. Eagerness about the morrow, fervor for responsibility, and zest for doing the small necessary things—these can only be sustained when the will has ordained a passion about the self.

Right here we begin, also, to note some difficulties. For nothing much happens merely because we are pleased by thoughts, even these thoughts. Despair about ourselves, augmented by our failures and fed by our guilt, lives in us when we try to will a passion and fail. Furthermore, ardent enthusiasm for being a distinctive self is often checked by the thoughts we have of ourselves, of our prospects, and of our own worth. It is almost as if our spirit becomes sick as our thought increases. Just as wisdom and moral doctrines seem cold and lifeless, so, too, our reflection about ourselves tends to make us indifferent and almost slothful. That passion for the good and for the self comes hard, at least when one has lived a bit and failed to succeed. The mood of despair is close to us much of the time.

Right at this juncture in a life history, Christianity has a great deal to say. For faith in God is also like a passion. Instead of being a natural disposition and a natural proclivity—a will to save one's life that can easily be frustrated and sidetracked—Christian passion is like a new capacity, a proneness, given to us from the outside. Faith itself is a gift, not another act of the natural will. We shall now see how this helps us make sense of ourselves, through a new will.

V

Christianity proposes a radically different point of departure for a new life. When we fail to make sense of our lives, the failure can be attributed much of the time to random and wayward emotions and also to the absence of virtue, to vices and moral formlessness. In the familiar human muddle, seriousness about willing one's redemption looks like the way to make one's life worthy again. This should not be overlooked or dismissed out of hand. Immense reservoirs of human potential can be realized. A certain delight in the law was remarked upon by a psalmist centuries ago. To bring wishes and wants into conformity with precepts and rules is to bring good sense into most lives. When one does that with ardor and enthusiasm, when one wills it easily, then one is entitled to a kind of contentment about oneself. If we are always at war with ourselves, so that our impulses are to do one thing and our thought is to do another, then the will is not a good one. Moral cultivation is something none of us can neglect, and surely we all stand to gain just in learning to will gladly what we must. Yet even with all its seriousness, this is not quite the Christian way.

Christian nurture proposes something else. It is that God also has a will and that we can know it and share it. There are many attributes of God that we do not know, at least if we take the Christian Scriptures seriously. But to know his will is not completely beyond our capabilities. More than this, it is by sharing his will that we approach God. Part of the meaning of being far from God is not geographical or physical distance but a matter of not willing as God wills. Physically speaking it must be that God is equally near to all, but, thinking now in moral and religious terms, some persons are nearer than others. Certainly we have to be careful here lest we begin to think that certain groups or especially pious emphases spell privilege before God. No, this is not the case. We must give full credit to the thought that a kind of righteousness is given us by God and that the divine initiative deserves all the praise. But still, people do have to choose the Christian way. They have to turn around and stay turned around.

What is involved is daring to let God and God's will govern and discipline my life when I tend to botch the job. That is a matter of giving up my willing and giving God's will the energizing role. Earlier we spoke of the fact that much of the Bible, not least the writing of Paul the apostle, is clearly on the side of proposing a kind of passive righteousness, given by God, as a means of justifying and saving our lives. This comes very close to being the heart of the gospel. We return to it in this different context. I do not have to depend wholly upon an activity of my will, as an energy that brings a passion to fruition, for now something different is at work: a God whose will is active on my behalf. God wills my redemption and gives me the conditions for savoring it. And in respect to that will, I, at least, do not have to constitute it by willing it (as I do my own will). To that extent I am passive in respect to the divine will. But I can now will, and hence be active again, because of his will.

The curse for all of us can be compounded by moral failure, guilt, weakness of will, and the breakdown of the very strength in which our character inheres. This is what happens when the frightful mood of despair takes over. Then one is unable to will any more. That is why despair so quickly becomes a kind of sloth and a disinclination to care and even to try. Hardly anyone despairs, deeply at least, until one has tried to make sense morally. Then it is as if one is dogged by one's earnestness and more deeply wounded because one has tried so intently.

This is all the more reason why Christian faith is for the brokenhearted. It proposes that the failure and weakness of the will is now a genuine experience, and that the good will that keeps willing the one thing needful is elusive. But more, instead of having passion spasmodically and having it vacillate between boredom and disinterest, the Christian design is a new kind of heartiness, a new passion, created by the will of God. So, if one knows what God is—a lover of all of us in our misery, but one who, nonetheless, has willed our happiness and a new life for each of us—then faith in that will be a passion. By choosing to live in God's will, we can find that God really begins to live within us. When we make our will in accord with his, our hope of glory gets a new foundation. Besides, God's nearness becomes a fact; we literally live no longer simply by ourselves, but Jesus Christ begins to live within us.

In order to make sense of our potentiality, we have to constitute it by willing. Of course, that is taxing, but also exceedingly worthwhile. It is little wonder that moral passion, a zeal for service, for community, for duty, and for making oneself can be heartening and hold the promise of a truly good life. If this way were smooth and safe, there surely would be no role for a Savior or for God. It is because that very moral passion produces guilt (indirectly, to be sure), perhaps a consciousness of sin, and perhaps, too, the despair we have noted, that another passion is called for. What the ancient world called prudence or wisdom, the fourth of the cardinal virtues, is fairly well summarized as the range of capacities to indulge human powers and to bring all of them to significant human practice. Much of the moral passion we have noted could be included under this wisdom. The Scriptures will have it that such wisdom is not radical or deep enough.

So by living with the consciousness that God is truly my friend, that his will is powerful and strong and never frustrated by guilt or despair, I can find a new stream of life. Faith in such a God is a passion. Everything that I am, that the world is, that the stream of life now provides, gets a new definition. I can now relish my days because victory is ahead. It follows that with such a God so near us, as close as the song in our hearts and the words on our lips, a new life can surge up in us. Then, too, we begin to love as God loves. No wonder that with a will now constituted by God's will, we can live again with real relish. Certainly a will like that will bring sense to a whole life.

CHAPTER FIVE

MAKING SENSE
WITH ONE'S THOUGHTS

I

It has been a long-time prejudice (an idea we refuse to think about!) to assume that the mind is the chief energy that allows persons to make sense. The presumption seems always to be that we make sense when we clearly articulate an idea or when we propose a theory. It is the idea or the thought, the argument or the theory, that is the bearer of meaning. Whatever sense is then being made is principally a function of thought in some kind of logical connection, or of language in some kind of grammatical arrangement, or both.

We have been projecting another range of considerations in these pages, namely, that persons themselves can be deprived of sense, that lives can be invalid, that you and I can be justified, that something besides language can be the bearer of sense, order, significance, and even truth. It is almost as if what the learned for centuries have called logical predicates, that is, what can be affirmed or denied about propositions or sentences, can be used somewhat like predicates about persons. Of course, we have to be careful here. Nothing is being said against logic or against the notion that language or thoughts ought to be clear, logically connected, or the bearers of sense. We cannot tolerate nonsense intellectually or allow chaos in our thought life. In addition, predicates change somewhat when they are moved from describing language to describing people. So one must not be taken in by the fact that the same word is being used in two different contexts and assume thereby that the meaning is identical.

Our point rests on something else. It is that not all of the sense made by persons emotionally, morally, or with the will is simply borrowed from the sense that is already embedded in objective truths, teachings, and arguments and realized by our intellectual endeavors. We have said repeatedly that sense is made with and by the emotions, with and by the will, with and by the virtues. Now we want to add that sense is made with and by our thoughts. But differences must be discerned in the area of our life where thought is central. Instead of always insisting that our intellect or our reason works only to articulate truths and to declare beliefs, which we then entertain and respond to by willing, behaving, and developing emotions, we want here to insist that the intellect is more intimate and even more direct in its effects. We make sense intellectually when we become scrupulous, clear, critical, and disciplined in daily life. We are subject here to modifications, to changes, and to being formed by thoughtfulness and careful consideration. Christianity indeed can be summarized in doctrines—that is not being denied—but Christianity is also a discipline and a teaching that modifies our thought life by securing our attention, by shaping us as intelligent beings. It does this to our intelligence by analogy with the way it produces new emotions in us. The Christian corpus of teachings, practices, sacraments, and worship generally will indeed contain theories and allow for all kinds of new ones. However, we must not neglect the plain fact that without Christianity most of us will also be tempted to make travesties of ourselves intellectually. We easily become believers in vanities and students of fads; we are tossed hither and yon by winds of doctrine; our intellects then become our undoing and our lives reflect the follies of worldliness. We seem to have forgotten that Christianity also reforms wayward minds and keeps them from making our lives wayward.

So, Christianity is also the training of our thoughts. We are modified by learning to think as Christians. Then our personality is subtly but firmly refashioned. However, this does not happen easily. In what follows, we will look at a kind of temptation that seems always available, the temptation to bring about the Christian transformation by sidestepping the intellect altogether. There is a kind of Christian anti-intellectualism that is born out of some of the misgivings we have stated above. We will begin by looking at that anti-intellectualism.

II

What many of us can know if we look around the gamut of Christian practices today—namely, a variety of attitudes toward beliefs, theology, and a distinctive thought content—can probably be read out of almost any period of religious history. There are those for whom the chief religious concern seems to be the cultivation of a range of experiences. These can be highly informal and episodic, or they can be highly formal and a matter of careful design. Usually the latter are part of a rich liturgical tradition, and the experiences that people can enjoy there are often esthetic and intentional. The more informal kinds are often deemed to be evidence of immediate visitations of the Holy Spirit. Frequently, these types of religiosity make theology almost useless and make thought almost an embarrassment or a hindrance to vivid faith. Certainly, in either of these alternatives there is frequently a fund of zeal for the things of God. Fortunately, most enthusiasts like these often find it necessary to be disciplined by the Scriptures; happily, too, most liturgical zealots are convinced that a theological order lies deep within the practice of Christian worship. Oftentimes, however, the life of thought and the activity of thinking are put in a subordinate place. Christian concepts are neglected while Christian experiences are eagerly sought.

Nonetheless, it does not seem adequate just to leave matters there. Both moral and Christian teachings address people in a rich variety of ways. The many-sided features of Christian teachings are appropriate to the complexity of persons, too. After all, each of us is a synthesis, a living synthesis of thought and pathos; of affection, will, and reflection; of purpose, hope, judgment, and memory. Some of us are richer in one respect than another, but all of us have to think about ourselves and the world, to plan our days, to sustain some pleasures, and to secure our worth. We are here arguing that our will, emotions, behavior, and thought can all be disciplined and trained by that complex called Christianity.

Putting these concerns in another form, we can say that Christianity can be assimilated and taken into one's life stream in a variety of ways. Not least, we can confront Jesus Christ as a historical person; what is essential to know about him can be stated in a collection of beliefs. Even God can be thought about. It is simply not true that everything Christian comes as a dramatic and overwhelming experience. Instead, there is much of the faith that is piecemeal, that comes more slowly and carefully, and that is encountered only when we think. We must dare also to think with the mind that is nurtured in us by Scripture, worship, and the Lord Jesus Christ.

Another note must be struck also, if only to do justice to the sheer romance and lovely grandeur of Christianity. One of the tragedies that any one of us can suffer can also be consequent to our thought life. For one thing, we can fail utterly as persons if we never learn to think at all. Pascal, that fascinating mathematical genius, physicist, and religious writer of the seventeenth century, said, with perhaps a little exaggeration, that though a drop of water or a reed might kill a man, he is more noble than that which slays him, because he, at least, knows that he dies. All of humanity's glory, Pascal insists, is in thinking. The negative of thought can be seen when we know someone who has no memory of the past, who does not evaluate his or her future, who never plans, proposes, or has views on much of anything. Such a person loses quality, and all human distinctiveness soon disappears. One becomes rudderless and a kind of waif.

For the facts about ourselves are that each is an original edition; each is born and dies at a specific time and in particular circumstances; each of us has the opportunity to forge a slant on life, a view of life, that will make a difference in our way of life. We all confront mysteries and problems. Some of them we can adjust to, others we can solve, but both suppose that we think. Thinking is a richly variegated activity (or a host of activities). It includes silent pondering of possibilities, careful consideration of consequences, deft skill in answering questions, nimble use of words, picturing oneself and one's prospects, and also seeing oneself in the context of the world.

Christianity is not like the weather, which most of us learn simply to undergo and to suffer. We encounter the weather and we can even learn from the weather, and that is because it is something to experience, to meet with, and to confront. If Christianity were only an experience, something to undergo, maybe to relish and savor as a taste or as a flow of pleasures, then we might indeed learn a little, but we would not find Christianity to be a way in which a self could become a new creature, in which a new life could be forged, and in which everything, early and late, mine and yours, could be gathered up and considered in its totality as a world.

Christianity is not just an event, not just a tissue of practices and observances, not just a culture or an institution; nor is it merely a body of discourse. If it were just these, it would be there, objectively, like the weather, waiting to be experienced. Instead, Christianity, while including church, teachings, historical events, and persons, is, as the New Testament so poignantly shows, an access and means to a new love, a new hope, a new way, and a new view—a new thought—about oneself, God, and the world. In short, not only is one educated and disciplined in order to become a Christian (that surely is needed by all of us), but one also is educated and trained, disciplined and built up *by* Christianity. The Christian life is a way to learn new emotions, new virtues and righteousness, a new will, and a novel and tough way of thinking about oneself, God, and the world.

One cannot deny the role of experience in Christian life. There are all kinds of crucial encounters when one meets the solemnity of great cathedrals, the sweep of doctrinal history, the survival value of powerless churches in world history, the heroism of martyrs and saints, and the spine-tingling choruses of Christian music. There is a wealth of experience to be had around Christian things. But if it is all at the expense of Christian understanding, of a deeply modified Christian thoughtfulness, then the truly high calling that is in Christ Jesus has been missed. For Christian faith also entails that one be converted in thought. It goes without saying, then, that one must have thoughts in order that they, too, be converted. So, we will now insist, Christianity is also a way to make sense intellectually. It is commensurate with what people are.

Just how the Christian passion enables us to make sense of our thoughts is not easy to say. If we have made anything of this discourse thus far, it is probably to the effect that Christianity cannot happen to us in one dramatic and devastating experiential moment. Because we are thoughtful, we are not dependent upon God as if he were an immense and random accident, a kind of massive happening. To be a Christian is to be tied up in God's promises, to be host to new expectations, and to be moved by a kind of divine love. The texture of one's life gets very rich. All kinds of new concepts are launched into our life history by such a skein of considerations.

Distinctive Christian concepts such as "God," "sin," "hope," "love," and "repentance" do not have significance only on paper or in pages like these. Instead, such concepts work in our very persons and in radical and unexpected ways. They help us to become considerate of ourselves and others, by conceiving of persons as children of God and by understanding any single life as a gift to be tendered in trust to its author, God. Already one's thought and life and one's conceptions are being subtly changed. Though Christianity is not initially only an experience, it becomes a momentous experience as new hopes grip us, as the passion of faith is eagerly willed, and as the new concepts help us to form a mind like that in Christ Jesus. Those concepts are the means by which this is effected. So now we turn to a consideration of what they are.

One of the chief ways that Christianity helps us build our lives is by giving us some of those new capacities we call "concepts." This may sound strange and formidable, almost too intellectual to be a part of faith and too aristocratic to be open to everyone, as Christianity proposes to be. But such considerations are a little premature, and they suppose an abstractness and technicality that is not intended at all. For concepts are not that strange, and clearly they are not alien to any one of us.

As we mature intellectually, we typically begin by learning words and a very simple use for them. Most children learn to ask, "What's that?" The answer is usually a word, used as a name. Most names answer questions like "Who is that?" or, more commonly, "What's that?" Seemingly everything and everybody can be identified with a name; and we know and think of the multitude of things, persons, and objects around us far better when we can give them their designations. Though naming is elementary, it is not altogether simple. For the singular question "What's that?" can be answered after a while in a number of ways. I can be looking at that shiny object on the table and say that it is a box or that it is brass, a square, a thing, or a mirror; furthermore, it is a thing, not a person; it is mine, not yours; it is metal, not wood. That simple object answers to many different ways of asking the question "What's that?" This is not only because the box is complex, constituted by material, shape, use, and ownership; it is also because people are very complex and they grow, socially and intellectually, so that they have at their command many ways to perceive, handle, and think about almost anything, including a square brass box. Much of what we mean by intellectual growth is summarized in an account like this. For human thoughtfulness is not simply a matter of knowing a great number of things; rather, it is a matter of acquiring a large number of capacities.

Once more we are up against a formidable-sounding word, "capacities." But it is not so difficult after all. When a child can begin to see that a box is also brass, shiny, and square, that child has been empowered somehow, has become able to see, to understand, and to appreciate in a richer variety of ways. The enabling, the empowering, and the skill in discernment are capacities. Such capacities are not in words or in talk or in one's eyes; they belong to the person, and they, in effect, lie behind the words and the eyes. When people become capacitated, they become able in certain definable ways, to see, to know, to hear, and to talk. Even what starts as simply naming this thing or that can grow into something rather impressive. This is because capacities are being stimulated.

When we speak of educating one another and helping someone in intellectual growth, we are not talking about simple addition. There are long books and endless lists of facts, but quantitative considerations soon come to an end once we have to educate another person. For people need more than facts, books, and data; they also need to be trained to discern and to see, to like what is likable, to dislike what is distasteful, to understand and, also, to understand what it means not to understand. Not least, they must be helped to know that even the square brass box is all kinds of things, depending on condition or use. Words have to be used in a variety of ways. All of what we have noted here supposes that there are capacities to be attained and powers to be realized. What we mean by being trained in thought can be illustrated by the above. It is the *person* who is becoming something—thoughtful, careful, precise, considerate, and wary of similarities and differences. A person has to be constituted and enabled. We are educating best when we help make people rational, discerning, and responsible. People are the target.

This is still only the beginning. We started by considering how words can be taught, not just as sounds but as names for things. Make no mistake, even that supposes a capacity, realizable in the life stream of a child. If a child is not able to do that, learning stops very soon. But now we press on to the more tangled issue of concepts. Already we have noted that capacities are involved. At the very least, we can say that a concept gets its somewhat exalted status by being a kind of capacity. There is something remarkable about a conceptual ability, as has long been observed. Let us go back to the earlier example of a child having its question "What's that?" answered by the expression "Box." After a while that word "box" is no longer just a name for a particular object; it becomes a more general word that is used to classify and to arrange all kinds of things, square, oblong, paper, brass, big, and small. This turns a name, which is specific, into a concept, which is general.

Another capacity has been realized in the child. It now sees boxes everywhere; it can find boxlike objects in a variety of circumstances. Soon even that word changes. Once it had a specific referent, but now it has a huge range of possible referents. What was once a word used only as a name is now a word exercised as a concept. So it happens with "man," "dog," "water," "brat," and most other names too. The growth is an intellectual one, indeed, a growth in the child. And this is no small matter. If it does not happen to a child, then a great deal of intellectual life is cut off rather sharply. We need such conceptual capacities to see how the world hangs together, to have almost any kind of knowledge, and surely to make sense of the world around us. The very rhythms and patterns of life, the things that belong to classes and kinds, the very appreciation of nature and its regularities and its accidents—all these require a conceptual ability. Most of us get so used to that capacity that we hardly realize its force in our lives. But we certainly can notice it quickly enough when it is absent.

Concepts, we have said, are powers that we exercise. They are in people. We need not invoke any special view of life to admit that point. Those concepts are not just general words; they are the abilities that enable us to use words correctly and with generality. There is a great deal more, too, as we will note subsequently. The point we are after here is that a human life is very dependent upon the acquisition of those capacities. This is not only a matter of words. Every person needs such abilities, and most of us in fact do acquire them. Without elaborate learning and a lot of detail, most of us get to know that birds are birds and people are people. We do not get lost simply in living things; we have long since separated world from self, earth from sky, and the living from the dead. We recognize a host of differences and myriads of similarities. Much of this conceptual capacity has been borne in upon us by thinking that is not sophisticated or even very apparent. This, however, is but more testimony to how dependent we are upon concepts and the thinking that concepts enable us to do.

Whether such thinking is intentional or unintentional, we all owe it a large debt. We can hardly call using names "thinking." Having names for things is more like a necessary preparation for thinking, but it is not quite thinking itself. We begin to think when we have concepts well-established in our repertoire. We cannot begin to have views, articulate a hope for ourselves, make a judgment of utility or inutility, or use words with scope and power until we have concepts at work. Surely, our plans and purposes presuppose a grip on large tracts of the future, just as our memories, our shame, and our remorse require a corresponding hold on major sweeps of our past. Even the recognition of past, present, and future bespeaks a major capacity. It is hard to see how a life can make sense if one has not made peace with one's past and made plans for the present and future. Concepts are involved, however, at every step.

We can conclude with Pascal that whatever distinctive glory is ours, we will not have it if we are thoughtless and stripped of the capacities that make up our thinking. If that happens, we will be real drifters again, hapless and helpless to find our way and quite unable to describe even our own case. In order to know who one is and what one should decide, one has to be able to think. And one cannot think if the capacities are missing.

III

The consequential issue is now before us: Nurture in things Christian is also nurture of the mind. That happens because some new abilities, some new concepts, which we have already named "capacities," are also grafted onto us. We must not forget that these capacities can be veritably life-giving. Without them we are stripped of the power to understand ourselves, the world around us, and our destiny. Admittedly this is a big claim. We shall seek to show how and why this is true.

Remember here that capacities are a property of the person, not of language, thoughts, doctrines, or theories. It is the person who is strengthened; and, some capacities being what they are, it is also the thinking of the person that is disciplined and augmented. Among the strengths gained is, of course, a kind of theoretical and doctrinal ability. Perhaps not every Christian feels the need to get every reflective issue straightened out and ordered in relation to God and the end of time. But Christians can conceive doctrinal schemes that sweep up the range of circumstances into some kind of rational outlook.

Typically, those capacities, grounded in the person, ought to engender and authorize large-scale thinking; this ought to be the case rather than large-scale thinking thriving on its own. One of the rebukes delivered to theology in the past has been its abstruseness and remoteness. That can scarcely be denied. But the difficulty for many has been that those thoughts could only be simulated and known at second hand if the religious capacities were not already present. To read from a page such grand thoughts and such magnificent language, when one's own form of life was not prepared for it at all, would make such thinking a rhapsody, at best, or a lot of intellectual nonsense, at worst. The Christian point in all this has a logical bite to it. We are required first to be changed, to be converted, as persons, to have something formed in us, before we can even make sense. This is true intellectually, too. We have to be able to match the thoughts.

Thus there is a general logical point about thinking that Christianity helps us to bring into focus. Because Christianity puts so much stress on the quality of the person, it does not permit us to believe that our thinking exempts us from this requirement. Our thinking and its qualities are also disposed by what we are as persons. There is a reproof in all this of thinking religiously at second hand, of collecting Christian ideas as if they were idle artifacts, or of presuming that because we can put words on our lips or on the page, we are entitled to the status of a Christian and a thinker. The priorities are clear once one sees what Christianity is. There are hollow people in intellectual circles, people whose lives make no sense even if they talk big. Christianity asks about the quality of one's life. This query is foremost, but it would do little good if it came to us only as one more requirement and if there were no way to meet it. It would be something like one more moral demand with no strength to meet it, or like the command to love God with all one's heart, soul, mind, and strength with no clue about how to go about it. Our point is that Christianity is not only a request for integrity in thought; it is, in itself, the very means of realizing that request. For there are Christian concepts. They do capacitate a person, but one must learn to let them take root and grow. Nurture is essential.

This is to assert that persons can and do make sense even in the world of thought. We have already remarked upon the difficulty of achieving self-knowledge. The difficulty is not that the self is so spiritual that it cannot be seen; rather, it is that there is no self there to know. We get something to know, discriminate, and understand when we begin to love deeply and long, to sorrow richly, to remember with constancy, and to behave temperately, justly, and courageously.

Now we can say something about what conceptual powers can add to all this. For one thing, the very notion of a self or soul is a heavily endowed Christian concept. Christianity does not let us rest with the easier concept of being an individual. That concept we can get by looking at one another and thinking about all the differences. We are numerically distinct; common sense and secular learning can easily help us find the concept of "individuality." It is a natural notion and not to be scoffed at, but it is not the same as the concept of the self or of the soul. Christianity teaches us to conceive of ourselves as being of infinite worth, and of God as one who cares for each of us and discerns our distinctive qualities, judges us, and even redeems us. This concept of the self is chiefly a product of our concern about what we are, and it grows with the kind of moral cultivation and willing we have noted. The very idea is supposed and enveloped by the notion of soul, for that is what we are when viewed by God Almighty.

More especially, though, we get a peculiar and powerful thrust in the direction of self-understanding, of knowing what it is to be a soul (as it were, a Christian person), when we construe ourselves as sinners. Now we really begin to attack and dismantle our pride. Not much else in the world will get at the very factor that keeps us from self-honesty and self-perspicuity. A good part of the ailment of human thinking is a consequence of pride. We begin to treat ideas and theories as if they were extensions of ourselves. We acquire what is called "vested interests," and none is any greater than pride or self-defense. The more pride one has, the more vulnerable one is. Soon even the slightest form of self-honesty becomes painful. Pride is usually fed by all the differences we can enjoy between ourselves and others. That there are differences cannot be denied, but pride causes us to make those differences even larger and to blur all the advantages that rightfully belong to others. Pride keeps us from giving evidence its true role and also from correcting ourselves frequently. It makes us stubborn, determined, and sure that we are right. We cannot afford even to be corrected, let alone wrong.

Then along comes Christian teaching, which says blandly that all have sinned and fallen short of the glory of God. It is one thing to know that phrase; it is another to let that concept of sin work its way into one's thought about oneself and others. Once it gets a hold, though, all kinds of things begin to look different. Imagine, for a moment, what the notion of being a sinner can do to one's pride! The concept of sin tells us immediately how we are before God. Here pride and self-aggrandizement simply have no status at all. God sees us as we are, and he can also easily lump us with others. We are part of the class called sinners. When one gets a little at ease in the notion of being a sinner, the differences between one-self and others begin to lose their status. Then one is not quite so impressed with one's differences or so thrilled by others' lapses or failures. One's thinking about oneself is now given a new authority and maybe even a bit of honesty.

It is a rather sad commentary on the human race that so many people are impressed with psychoanalysis. That set of doctrines and therapy simply assumes that most people cannot even begin to know themselves by themselves. And it takes many hours of a professional's time, and a great deal of money, plus a painful reconstruction of the patient's mental history, just to get one in the position of seeing correctly what one truly is. There must be hard cases when all this is justified, but certainly Christians could not admit that it has to be the general rule and method for all people. Christian teaching would have it that a regeneration of one's thought is also to be acquired in religious nurture. For the working of grace actually creates in us the concept of sin, a capacity that will permit us to see ourselves as God sees us. We can then think validly and powerfully about ourselves.

This is why we can say that Christianity enables us to make sense with our thoughts. Pride can distort thinking more quickly than can neglected evidence or a faulty inference. Most of us cannot judge the whole world and its circumstances morally, because we simply do not know enough. Therefore, each of us has to become just, so that however tentative our judgments are, and will necessarily be, the person making them will be morally sound. Something like this obtains in matters of thought, too. We cannot guarantee every thought and justify every inference. The relations between thoughts and the world are various and confounding. If sense depended only on command of the externals, all thinking would be like one wild guess after another. No, we also have to become honest and chaste in idea so that whatever thoughts we dare will be expressions of an honest and chaste thinker. It looks as though the Christian faith has made this available to all of us, whether our thought life be extensive and general, as it might be for a scientist or scholar, or particular and circumscribed, as it must be for most of us most of the time.

Something comparable could also be said about the several concepts tied up with the word "world." Certainly there is a concept here that we have all learned in the commonsense traffic of daily life. When I talk about the world in contrast to myself, I am commanding a rather large range of circumstances, phenomena, and things. The word is not very precise and is hard to define, but it bespeaks a very useful concept; not many confusions or mistakes are perpetrated by its use. The notion of "world" can be said to be necessary for much of everyday thinking, even though it is not taught us by any science or any religion. But Christianity has a way of pulling that word into another conceptual posture. The world is put together as the largest and most inclusive agglomerate—stars, earth, you and me—under the notion that all of it is created. None of it has to be; none of it is necessary. It is all made, and it is not permanent. It is all created and is something like a gift, to be cherished with gladness and used in remembrance of its giver. Now the contrast that we already know between ourselves and the world gets yet another component. The life of a human being was made for immortality and life eternal, but the duration of everything else is quite different. The world passes away, but persons actually do not. The contrast between oneself and other people and, on the other hand, the physical and social world now takes on a deeper significance. Another feature of all this is that instead of depending simply upon the world, physical or social, I as a Christian am now empowered by the concept of being a soul to learn to depend radically upon the author of everything that is.

Becoming worldly is something like a threat. The fact is, obviously, that most persons spend their lives becoming at home in the world. They seek to make themselves salable, they strive after reputation, they want power and money, all to get a little ease and satisfaction in the world. Furthermore, the work of the best minds, the consensus of every society, the drift of most thinking, and the weight of social institutions and personal habits are all on the side of domesticating all of us to the world around us. We become conformists. We also become restless, dissatisfied, and terribly busy chasing goals that prove to be evanescent anyway. Trying to become at home in the world is a full-time occupation. The Bible tells us—and we must be reminded again—that God has planted the eternal in our hearts. It should not surprise us, then, if we discover how hard we are to please. We stay restless in the world even with our successes.

It is one thing to learn all this in doctrines and general moralizing accounts. We can hear someone saying, "Stop preaching!" The summary accounts that we have given might also be supplemented by the story of the human race, from the day of creation to the second coming of Jesus, or it might be dressed out in a story of evolution, from a tiny cell, through countless permutations of species, to a consummation in one world at peace. Our point is that general accounts, whether biblical, scientific, or commonsense, do not change very much. We can entertain views endlessly; these days sophisticated people do this easily because print is cheap and quasi-learned talk is everywhere. If Christianity becomes only one more component in this endless proliferation of points of view, it will certainly be powerless. This is exactly what has happened with this explosion of learned talkativeness. Christian teachings have also entered this stream of plausible options and are entertained in the same genial way, as if they are interesting, one more possibility, one idea among many.

What has been forgotten in all this is precisely that the intellectual content of Christianity is not handled at all accurately and aptly if it is done by analogy with all the other hypotheses the race has invented. For Christianity is not just a complex of ideas to be entertained. It is rather a power of God working in us. We have tried to indicate this by alluding to the rich emotional content it can produce, the charismatic virtues it can evoke, and the determination to will one thing that it plants in us. Now it can be said that there are Christian views, but we have added that there are Christian concepts too. And those concepts do not work only in making points of view. They work in ourselves, enabling us to see differently and even to behave differently. They are a new power in us.

On the issue of getting a grip on the scene around us, Scripture says that it is all created, a kind of creature. Perhaps it might suddenly occur to you, as you think about yourself, how silly it is to be too dependent upon the world, to worry about succeeding in it, when it too will pass away. In a thousand ways, in an almost indefinite range of uses, that concept "world," used Christianly, now gives you what the New Testament calls freedom or liberty. You are no longer in bondage, no longer a slave, no longer a worldling. Whereas our daily life and most learning that we come across tend to make us ever more dependent upon the world and correctly knowing it, Scripture frees us from the world. The point is exactly this, that Christian learning is something wonderful in you that now empowers you to forge your own freedom from the world. In ways like this, those Christian concepts make our minds independent and even rather dauntless. The eternal planted in the human heart now gets something to work with.

Concepts like justification, redemption, and being "born again" can be deployed so that the human mind is strengthened and freed up for the true romance of being a person. The mind is given some muscle by which it can help us understand ourselves, the world, and God's interest in us. All this has been said only because thinking and being rational are such precarious things. Most of the intellectual rubbish that permeates the world and most of the truly big mistakes in policy and thought have been made by smart people. And the criteria for thought that are supposedly intrinsic to thought, that are articulated by thinking itself, are quite helpless in stemming the tide of nonsense. None of us can afford to think lightly of such logical criteria as consistency, exactness, and noncontradictoriness, but it is sobering and humbling to remember that these are, by and large, quite irrelevant to the goodness or badness of humankind and that they cannot predispose us very far even in contrasting truth and error. We need another kind of strengthening of the inward person, of the thinking person. And this is what the life of Christian faithfulness promises.

IV

We have been using an old and distinctive set of categories—thoughts, virtues, emotions, and the will—to address some very old concerns. Those issues are roughly that both religion and morals are matters of practice, somehow consequent to theory or to something like a theory. Obviously in neither the moral nor the Christian enterprise is the word "theory" quite right. However, the distinction between theory and practice seems powerful today and applicable almost everywhere. Discourses that tell one what is right to do and Christian doctrines that catch up the main themes of Christianity are often conceived as theories, as if in all cases they precede the practice. Our purpose has been to say that this "theory-practice" distinction is misleading when we consider most moral and Christian matters. Such a distinction makes it seem as if all the sense is in the theory or the theology and all the practical application is in the emotions, the will, and the virtues. Rather, lives can begin to make sense via emotions, will, virtues, and thoughts, when all these are under Christian nurture.

If a theory tells us something, we can say that Christian

teachings are like theories in telling us something. I have not denied the long-standing theorem of thinking people that words can be about something, that propositions can give us the truth, and that in theological discourse we do have truths about God, Jesus, ourselves, and the world. But our stress has not been on this point, and details on the vindication and the logical character of theology must be left to be discussed in other places. Rather, it has been urged that other uses of moral and religious teachings properly came first. Instead of making theories and truth claims that we then consider (or perhaps entertain seriously), compare with modern science, make relevant in the twentieth century, doubt for a while, try to believe, and so on—instead of all that, we have treated theories as enabling us to become viable and persistent, stalwart survivors in daily life. The target of religious attention, the aim of it all, is to build up, to edify the person. And each person must learn, and can learn, how to make sense of life. It is not as if everything depends upon knowing first the teachings that are clearly true, then daring to indulge in a little practice. It is more like this, that the teachings along with worship really address us insofar as we have needs, and those needs can be for anything that does not allow us to make sense. These needs are often directly addressed. Perhaps in meeting them we will so build ourselves up that becoming certain of the truth will then become easier, just as becoming happier might also come within reach.

It goes almost without saying that if all this is relevant, then we have the whole person in focus. It is popular today to speak of holistic medicine and holistic psychology, and even of holistic religion. We can only hope that the term "holistic" will not have to be used at all once one surmises how many-sided and rich Christian cultivation actually is. For the manner in which the entire person is engaged is subtle, yet firm and unremitting. Begin with the emotion of hope, hope in God, and you will discover that the need to vanquish despair and to live hopefully will also begin to stimulate the need for a better concept of God. Most of us have hardly any concept of God at all, barely even an image or a vague intimation. But the exercise of hope in one's life, letting deep feelings grow as one centers down into steadfastness and patience, will cause the very idea of a God to take root too. And before long the hope that began as an emotion will become something like a moral habit, a truly charismatic virtue.

But it goes the other way, too. If one begins with a concept like that of the Christian God, then one is not only empowered to think about the real God (not a concept) but also empowered to become hopeful. Part of the exercise of that concept "God" is that it makes cowardliness, cringing, and halfhearted morality a downright embarrassment. We have said that concepts are abilities. The "God concept" (while, of course, enabling you to refer to God) creates in you the will to keep a promise, causes you misgivings about your own righteousness, and gives you a zest for the new righteousness that is a good part of the very content of the God idea. All these things mesh after a bit. So thoughts and emotions, virtues, and will are not quite separated factors or faculties after all. People will be whole and unitary, almost despite themselves.

There is a new life awaiting all of us in the assimilation of Christian nurture. The story of God's love and majesty, manifested in the creation of the world, in the life and death of Jesus, and in his resurrection, which is the promise of ours too, is a lovely backdrop for the human scene. We can spend ourselves in contemplating it from beginning to end, and perhaps take heart in the fantastic role we have in it, but we ought not to lose ourselves even in such a glorious story. We must live in the grace and the new motives that the story promises. In fact, if we do not find those new motives, new thoughts, emotions, habits, and a new will, it must be that we have not understood the story.